CRAFTY
Bastards

PRAISE FOR *CRAFTY BASTARDS*

"Journalist Lauren Clark's no-nonsense prose makes each fact pop, with the occasional wink at those 'quiet, resilient' New Englanders (comparing British soldiers at a patriots' tavern to Yankees in a Sox bar? Spot-on)."

—Courtney Cox, *Beer Advocate*

"Lauren Clark has written a charming history of New England 'suds'— beer, cider, ale, and any other alcoholic variations that could be made with locally grown grains, grasses, and stalks. It's a fascinating path that wanders from the very technical (yeast, alcohol content) to the political..."

—Louisa Kasdon, *edible BOSTON*

"Throughout this historic romp, the author deftly crams in as many tidbits as possible while weaving an engaging narrative, avoiding the stuffy tone that often accompanies history books ... Clark takes readers on an entertaining journey across five centuries of New England beer history, highlighting Yankee ingenuity as it relates to the region's beer-making heritage and present."

—Jim Baumer, *All About Beer*

"Reading each chapter of *Crafty Bastards* feels like a well-informed, sometimes wild, sometimes awkward conversation among a bunch of friends at a bar."

—Shaun Kirby, *RI Central*

"Clark travelled throughout New England to over 100 breweries to tell their stories. The book can also double as a beer-lovers vacation itinerary."

—Luke O'Neil, *Metro*

BEER IN NEW ENGLAND
from the MAYFLOWER TO MODERN DAY

LAUREN CLARK

Boston UNION PARK PRESS

Union Park Press
Wellesley, MA 02481
www.unionparkpress.com

Printed in U.S.A.
First Edition
10 9 8 7 6 5 4 3 2

Library of Congress Cataloging-in-Publication Data

Clark, Lauren (Journalist)
  Crafty bastards : the history of beer in New England from the Mayflower to modern day
/ by Lauren Clark. -- First edition.
      pages cm
   Includes bibliographical references and index.
   ISBN 978-1-934598-11-5 (paperback : alkaline paper)
   1. Beer--New England--History. 2. Breweries--New England--History. 3. Brewing
industry--New England--History. 4. Brewing--History. 5. Microbreweries--New England.
6. New England--Social life and customs. I. Title.
   TP577.C53 2014
   338.4'7663420974--dc23
                                    2014010246
ISBN: 978-1-934598-11-5
1-934598-11-9

Book and cover design by Vale Hill Creative. www.valehillcreative.com

Union Park Press titles are also available in a variety of digital formats. Please visit our
website to learn more: www.unionparkpress.com.

For Mom, Dad, and Harry Proudfoot

Brewers pose with barrels of beer at the Haffenreffer Brewery, courtesy of the Haffenreffer family.

CONTENTS

Introduction

In December 2012, I moderated an MIT Enterprise Forum discussion called "Brewing Up Bucks: The Business of Microbreweries." Owners of six Massachusetts craft breweries were there to talk about their companies. Martha Simpson-Holley chronicled the lean beginnings of her eclectic Pretty Things Beer and Ale Project, which she and her husband, brewer Dann Paquette, started with their life savings of eight thousand dollars. Drew Brosseau, a former software industry consultant who owns the Mayflower Brewery, told of the logistical challenges of packaging and distribution. Sam Hendler described the legal red tape that he and his brewer brother, Jack, encountered when they launched Jack's Abby, New England's first independent all-lager brewery since the Industrial Era.

The panelists made it clear that brewing isn't an easy business. And the amount of bucks being brewed up seemed somewhat less than tantalizing. Yet no one seemed discouraged. There was real enthusiasm in the room about the business of craft beer. When I asked how many in the audience were thinking of starting breweries, several people raised their hands. The panelists at times appeared incredulous at the level of interest in their industry from a crowd of mostly MIT students who would have many attractive career options post-graduation.

But maybe it shouldn't be surprising that those students could be as passionate as any other aspiring brewer. They came of age on a tidal wave of craft beer that has washed over New England during the past several years. It has caught even veterans of the industry by surprise. There are more breweries in the region than ever before—two hundred and counting. Some of those enterprises have been around since the first wave of microbreweries launched in the 1980s and 1990s, but many have sprung up within the past several years. None of the breweries on that 2012 panel were more than five years old. They're part of a nationwide resurgence of craft beer—that is, beer made with quality ingredients in relatively small batches and usually sold near where it's made.

When it comes to brewing, New Englanders have always been a uniquely scrappy, thirsty, and morally fraught bunch. The region is (aside from the Dutch-settled parts of New York) the oldest beer-drinking culture in the United States; and New England brewers have been shaped by four hundred years of overcoming adversity. They have survived and thrived despite scarce ingredients, competition from rum, the dominance of megabrews, and the microbrewery crash of the late 1990s. Forever battling the Puritan mentality that has always veered between encouraging and discouraging brewing in the region, these crafty bastards continue to ferment a distinctively Yankee beer culture, pint after savory pint.

———◇———

I briefly joined the ranks of New England brewers at the tail end of craft beer's first growth period. In 1996 I quit my desk job to become an apprentice at the Commonwealth Brewing Company in Boston. In operation from 1986 to 2002, the brewpub was the first craft brewery to open in New England, and it launched the careers of several accomplished brewers (more about that in chapter seven, *Yeast*).

I had been enthralled with microbrews since I became aware of the likes of Geary's, Sam Adams, and Catamount in the late 1980s. To a New Hampshire girl who came of age drinking Old Milwaukee and Molson Golden, those beers were revolutionary. They had... *flavor*! They were revivals of styles that had been presumed lost after decades of domination by light lager.

Fascinated, I started reading about beer history. I discovered that New England had a remarkably diverse beer market just before and after Prohibition. That's because it took longer for us than the rest of America to abandon our Old World ale and beer styles in favor of light lager. Rediscovering this bygone era of pale and brown ales, Bohemian pilsners and Vienna lagers, and stouts and bocks led me to experiments in homebrewing and, eventually, to see what it would be like to work in a craft brewery.

I showed up at the Commonwealth one day and asked head brewer Jeff Charnick*, a tall man with curly brown hair and glasses, if he was training interns. The next thing I knew, I was wearing tall rubber boots and scrubbing yeast residue off the walls of a stainless-steel fermenter. *Wow*, I thought. *I'm working in a brewery—in the basement of a restaurant!* People dining upstairs would soon be drinking pints of the delicious ale that had just drained from the tank in which I was standing. My compensation for cleaning and sanitizing was an education in English-style ale, along with access to a world of people who were, with little to no formal training, making a living as brewers.

Following my internship at the Commonwealth, I got a job as an assistant brewer at the Cambridge Brewing Company, a brewpub in

---

*Along with many other acquaintances of Charnick, I was shocked and saddened when he unexpectedly succumbed to a heart attack in 2010.

Cambridge that opened in 1989. Owner Phil Bannatyne and head brewer Will Meyers taught me how to make—and appreciate—the progressive styles in the pub's repertoire, including an early example of a double IPA, Red God, and America's first commercial Belgian-style tripel, Tripel Threat. It was fun while it lasted. When I landed at Cambridge Brewing I had already begun freelancing for the craft beer newspaper *Ale Street News*. After a couple of years of doing both, I decided I was more suited to writing about beer than brewing it.

As I made my transition from brewer to beer writer at the turn of the millennium, the first wave of craft beer had subsided. Many breweries had closed, and the excitement and growth the industry enjoyed in the 1990s had dampened. Nevertheless, insiders knew that craft beer wasn't going anywhere—contrary to mainstream commentators' pronouncements that it was a played-out trend. Around the country, the industry continued to grow. In New England, beer bars caught on, with brews from all over the United States and the world flowing through their taps. And then, finally, new brewing enterprises began to launch again in the region, and existing ones evolved.

Nowadays, wow—it's an embarrassment of riches out there. New craft breweries have found success, for example, in previously hard-to-crack areas, including White Birch in the Budweiser bastion of central New Hampshire and Two Roads, a cutting-edge contract-brewing facility in import-centric southwestern Connecticut. Midcoast Maine has a pair of groovy brewing ventures—the Belgian farmhouse-inspired Oxbow and Marshall Wharf in artsy Belfast—which are both worth a drive up from Portland. You can now find breweries everywhere, from a bucolic Trappist monastery in western Massachusetts to Trillium Brewery in the trendy Fort Point neighborhood in Boston.

Some say that the latest expansion of the craft sector is irrational exuberance all over again, that there are too many beers out there, and that we're headed for another crash like we had in the late 1990s. Maybe.

Of course there are still many more nooks and crannies in New England without a brewery than with one. Craft beer represents only 11 percent of nationwide beer sales, so there's plenty of room to grow. Plus, many of New England's successful brewers are veterans of the first wave or built their careers during the fallow post-crash years. They seem to have a typically Yankee sense of thrift and caution when it comes to running their businesses, even as they may push stylistic boundaries with their beer. For many of them, growth is not the holy grail as much as making a decent living and having some fun while selling beer to the local community. That was harder to do in the 1990s, when craft beer was an unknown category and brewers had to stretch outside their territory just to sell product. These days, more people are seeking out good, locally made beer, and many craft brewers are more than happy to serve a clientele close to home.

Brewing for one's community is where it all started. For the better part of New England's history, almost all beer was local. Puritan housewives, colonial tavern-keepers, and Industrial Age brewers made beer for their families, neighbors, or fellow city dwellers. In doing so, they created a vital heritage for our modern brewers. The story of how we got from there to here is an enlightening and interesting one, especially over a beer or two.

Water

Y ou know the joke about the guy ordering a glass of water at a bar and being served a light beer? For New England's early settlers, the punch line wouldn't have hinged on the shortcomings of the beer, but rather on the idea that anyone would seriously ask for a drink of water. Everyone knew water was poisonous. Beer (which is more than 90 percent water, after all) was the wholesome way to hydrate.

The British men and women who established the New England colonies in the 1600s came from a populated place where modern practices of sanitation were still centuries away. Drinking from common—and often polluted—water sources could make them sick, or worse. In short, plain water was not to be trusted. But when it was boiled in the process of making a mildly alcoholic beverage, it was rendered safe.

Beer *was* water. It was food, too. Early settlers considered the grain-based beverage nourishing—liquid bread—and drank it morning, noon, and night. There were different strengths of beer, ranging from strong beer, whose flavor and buzz-inducing qualities were as appreciated as any of today's craft brews, to small beer, a low-alcohol beverage that even children drank. Yes, children drank beer. There were no juice boxes back then, no sippy cups of milk (milk was made into cheese and butter). No soda, no sports drinks. No coffee, no tea (they were still decades away from wide availability). Beer was it—the universal beverage.

So, you can see why the Pilgrims, sailing through Cape Cod Bay in December of 1620, panicked a bit over their "victuals being much spent—especially [their] beere," as Plymouth Colony's governor, William Bradford, put it. Instead of heading south toward their preferred destination, the Hudson River, they parked the *Mayflower* in Plymouth Harbor and began to figure out how they were going

Governor John Winthrop, who enjoyed a "good venison pasty and good beer." Wood carving, 1860.

to make it through the winter. We all know the end of the story: the Pilgrims stuck around, learned from the Indians how to grow corn, and progressed from a starving and forlorn group of near-castaways to the first permanent settlement in the future United States.

What? The Pilgrims landed at Plymouth because they were low on beer? Yep. I know, my teachers never told me that either.

"Near-castaways" isn't much of a stretch in describing the Pilgrims. The *Mayflower's* crew was as concerned as their passengers about the ship's dwindling provisions; they needed to save some food and drink for their voyage back to England. So they kicked the Pilgrims off the ship and wished them luck.

You can imagine Bradford getting hot under the stiff collar as he relives that moment in his account of the Pilgrims' travails, *Of Plimouth Plantation*. He writes that he and his roughly one hundred companions "were hasted ashore and made to drink water that the seamen might have the more beere." When many of the Pilgrims started to get sick and starve, Bradford pleaded with the mariners for a small container of beer. Their response was that if Bradford "were their own father he should have none." Ouch.

It wasn't until the crew also began to succumb to disease—including scurvy, which beer was thought to prevent—that the *Mayflower's* captain relented and shared some of the ship's precious malt liquor. Nevertheless, by the time the winter of 1620-1621 was out, half of all those who had sailed to Plymouth on the *Mayflower* had died.

John Winthrop was not about to repeat that tragedy. In 1630, he was getting ready to lead his own band of Church of England dissenters, the Puritans, to Massachusetts Bay. Compared to the Pilgrims, the Puritans had their act together when it came to migration and settlement plans. To begin with, Winthrop outfitted his flagship, the *Arbella*, with the equivalent of ten thousand gallons of beer. For roughly four hundred passengers and crew on a two-month journey, that's about four pints per person per day. To your health!

And what was waiting for Winthrop when he reached Massachusetts Bay? Not the lonesome wilderness that the Pilgrims faced, but a cozy supper of "good venison pasty and good beer." That warm welcome was courtesy of John Endecott, the colony's first governor. He had led an advance group of settlers to Salem to make things homey for their fellow emigrants—people who left comfortable lives back in England to risk an ocean crossing and pin their futures on Winthrop's vision of a godly, shining city upon a hill.

Luckily, that city would have beer as soon as possible. Evidence shows that the English began brewing promptly after they set foot on these shores. Winthrop family letters from 1633 refer to malt and brewing equipment imported from Britain. That year also saw America's first licensed tavern, Cole's Inn, open its doors in Boston—one year after the first church and two years before the first school, Boston Latin. In 1637, the first commercial brewing license in the New World was issued to Captain Robert Sedgwick, a prominent citizen of Charlestown.

Meanwhile, Plymouth Colony, after surviving its first tough years, also made sure its citizens had something to drink. Tavern licenses were issued to Francis Sprague in Duxbury in 1638, Thomas Lumbert in Barnstable in 1639, and Richard Paul in Taunton in 1640. "It seems likely, in the absence of any contrary information, that many of the tavern keepers were their own brewers," writes Stanley Baron in *Brewed in America: The History of Beer and Ale in the United States* (1962).

———◆———

Rhode Island had to wait a few years for its first pint. Unlike previous New England settlements, it launched without any financial

*What Cheer! Roger Williams in Narragansett Bay, courtesy of
Roger Williams University Library.*

or political backing from the old country. Roger Williams moved
there after being been banished from Massachusetts by his fellow
Puritans, who disagreed with his views on religious freedom and his
disapproval of confiscating land from the Indians. The Indians, in
turn, traded him a piece of land on Narragansett Bay that he named
Providence. In one of the coolest moments in all of New England
history, the Narragansetts are said to have greeted Williams with,
"What cheer, netop?" Roughly: "What up, dude?" This story was

repeated from one generation to the next until "What Cheer" became the motto for the City of Providence (and the name of a pre-Prohibition brewery in Cranston.)

Once Williams recruited enough kindred rebels to Providence to fill a tavern, the first innkeeper and commercial brewer, Sargeant Baulston, hung out his shingle in 1639. Apparently, the beer supply was ample enough that by 1655, Rhode Island Colony's four towns (Providence, Portsmouth, Newport, and Warwick) decided that they should each have no more than two innkeepers. One of the earliest taverns in Rhode Island, the White Horse in Newport, opened in 1673 and is still serving beer today.

Records left by Connecticut's pioneers, who moved south from the Massachusetts Bay and Plymouth colonies in the 1630s in search of open land, indicate that they began homebrewing the instant they put roofs over their heads. They spent the early years of the colony in bloody conflict with the Pequot Indians and didn't build taverns—official ones, at least—until 1644. Connecticut's first commercial brewer, Stephen Goodyeare, set up shop in New Haven in 1646.

Before the Puritans lugged their bibles and brewkettles all over southern New England, beer was almost certainly being made in the settlement of Strawbery Banke, which began in 1631 in what would become Portsmouth, New Hampshire. This outpost had little to do with religion. It sprang from commercial fishing, lumber, fur, and shipping enterprises funded by investors back in England, namely Captain John Mason. Mason, who never set foot in Portsmouth, supplied his overseas stewards well, for an inventory taken in 1635 lists fifteen barrels of malt in Strawbery Banke's "great house." Early Granite State tavern licenses went to Robert Tuck of Hampton in 1638 and Henry Sherborne of Portsmouth in 1642. John Webster became the first licensed brewer in 1651 in order to sell beer on the Isles of Shoals, just off the coast of Portsmouth.

None of the aforementioned brewing enterprises were remotely large in scale. But given that they made it into the record books—most brewing activity didn't—it's clear that beer was quickly on its way to becoming as universal a beverage in the New World as in the Old.

Never mind that the water in the New England colonies was safe to drink. It was downright pristine, in fact. John Winthrop was a fan and, model citizen that he was, pretty much stuck to water after that initial beer at Endecott's house. He had already moved his settlement from Charlestown to the Shawmut Peninsula, where he founded Boston, because the latter had a nice natural spring.

William Wood, in a sort of early travel guide called *New England's Prospect* (1634), writes that "there can be no better water in the world" than that found in New England, and "those that drinke it be as healthfull, fresh, and lustie, as those that drinke beere." Nevertheless, knowing his audience back home, he prefaces his praise of Mass Bay's finest with "dare I not preferre it before good beere." He also urges those planning on making the voyage to the New World to bring their own malt with them.

William Bradford had similar backhanded compliments for New England water. In 1624, responding to those in England who questioned the wholesomeness of the native liquid, he writes, "If they mean, not so wholesome as the good beer and wine in London… we will not dispute with them. But else for water it is as good as any in the world."

Cultural habits don't change easily, and Winthrop and his fellow "healthfull, fresh, and lustie" water drinkers had little company. For the same reason that modern people, for example, continue to eat cheese even though refrigeration made it unnecessary to preserve milk by fermenting it, the English men and women who ventured across an ocean and started a new civilization stuck with beer. It made them happy.

——◆——

In the typical upper-middle-class English household of the colonial period—the type of household most Puritans came from—providing the family's essential beverage was a woman's job. Women brewed the beer, served the beer, drank the beer, and even mixed the beer with herbs to make medicine. It's hard for modern folk to imagine, as we know beermaking as an industrial activity run almost wholly by, and for, men. That state of affairs took hold when brewing became a large-scale, profitable enterprise, around 1700 or so in England and quite a bit later in America.

Before that, it was one of a woman's many, many household tasks, along with churning butter, spinning wool, planting vegetables, managing livestock, and so on—the likes of which were laid out in instructional books (written by men). Thomas Tusser's *Book of Housewifery* in the late 1500s and Gervayse Markham's *The English Housewife* (1615) are two examples.

Note the first item in Tusser's list of routine housewifely duties: "Brewing, Baking, Cookery, Dairy, Scouring, Washing, Dinner Matters, Afternoon Works, Evening Works, Supper Matters, After-Supper Matters." His guide is full of pithy little rhymes that both tell a woman how to do her work and affirm the worthiness of her labor. Here's one on brewing:

Brew somewhat for thine
else bring up no swine.

In buying of drink, by the firkin or pot
the tally ariseth, but hog amends not.
One bushel well brewed, outlasteth some twain
And saveth both malt, and expenses in vain.

Too new is no profit, too stale is as bad
drink dead or else sour makes laborer sad.

Remember good Gill
take pain with thy swill.

Seeth grains in more water, while grains be yet hot
and stir them in copper, as porridge in pot.

In other words, brew beer because it's cheaper than buying it, and you can feed your pigs the spent grain. (Livestock enjoy that leftover grain even today.) If you brew carefully, you won't waste malt or wind up with beer that's too young or gone sour. And don't forget to make a second (weaker) brew using the grains from the first.

Making one or two successively weaker batches of beer by adding new water to the same pot of malted grain was standard practice in both British and American brewing up until the twentieth century. Today, most brewers use up all the sugars in the grain in just one brew by sparging, or sprinkling additional water on the malt after its initial soak.

In Markham's *The English Housewife*, there are no cute rhymes—he's all business. He gives detailed instructions on making "ordinary" and "strong" beer, as well as on malting barley, beer's primary grain. To put it very simply, malting involves steeping grain in water just until it begins to sprout, then heat-drying it so that you end up with little pellets of powdery starch that yeast can ferment. It's actually a multi-step process that takes several days. Markham declares that malting is "properly the work and care of a woman, for it is a housework. The man ought only to bring in and to provide the grain."

Just reading Tusser and Markham's checklists of a housewife's duties makes me tired. And I can't even imagine the difficulty of trying to keep up with the brewing, the baking, and the after-supper matters while living in early New England, with its harsh winters and Indian wars. Housewives probably weren't too brokenhearted when men unburdened them of the task of brewing by transforming it into an industrial enterprise.

But that transformation took time, and brewing remained on the housewife's docket in rural areas well after the American Revolution, as we see in Lydia Maria Child's *American Frugal Housewife*, published in the 1830s. Abolitionist, women's-rights activist, and author of "Over the River and Through the Wood," Child grew up in Medford, Massachusetts. As if the title of her book weren't Yankee enough, she gave it this subtitle: "Dedicated to those who are not ashamed of economy."

Her section on brewing begins, "Beer is a good family drink." She then proceeds with instructions for making beer that only the most tightfisted, eccentric Yankee would inflict upon her family.

> A handful of hops, to a pailful of water, and a half-pint of molasses, makes good hop beer. Spruce mixed with hops is pleasanter than hops alone… Malt mixed with a few hops makes a weak kind of beer; but it is cool and pleasant; it needs less molasses than hops alone. The rule is about the same for all beer. Boil the ingredients two or three hours, pour in a half-pint of molasses to a pailful, while the beer is scalding hot. Strain the beer, and when about lukewarm, put a pint of lively yeast to a barrel. Leave the bung loose till the beer is done working; you can ascertain this by observing when the froth subsides… A raw potato or two, cut up and thrown in, while the ingredients are boiling, is said to make beer spirited.

About the molasses: it turned out to be a much more common fermentable material in New England than barley. About the raw potato: your guess is as good as mine.

Some Yankee women brewed commercially; the old English word for them was brewster. Sister Bradish of Cambridge, Massachusetts, is an interesting example, because her name comes up in a case before the Middlesex County Court in 1654.

Bradish sold bread and "penny beer" to Harvard students and was apparently a great comfort to the lads, who would have arrived on campus at roughly age sixteen to prepare for careers as Puritan

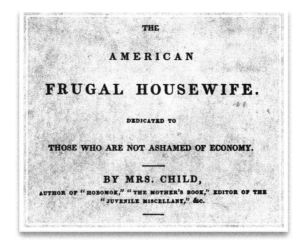

THE

AMERICAN

FRUGAL HOUSEWIFE.

DEDICATED TO

THOSE WHO ARE NOT ASHAMED OF ECONOMY.

BY MRS. CHILD,

AUTHOR OF "HOBOMOK," "THE MOTHER'S BOOK," EDITOR OF THE "JUVENILE MISCELLANY," &c.

Mrs. Child's "The Frugal Housewife" was later reprinted as "The American Frugal Housewife." Those who are not ashamed of economy continue to enjoy it.

ministers. Maybe she was like a diner waitress who called everybody "honey" and wished them luck on their ancient-Greek test. In any case, some parents complained that she was "harbouring students, unseasonably spending their time and parent's estate," according to a letter written by Harvard president Henry Dunster to the court on Bradish's behalf. He was having none of the parents' accusations.

"I found it a misinformation," he assured the jurors. Not only that, he asked that Bradish "might be encouraged and countenanced in her present calling for baking of bread and brewing and selling of penny beer … Such is her art, way and skill, that she doth vend such comfortable penniworths for the relief of all that send unto her, as elsewhere they can seldom meet with." Plus, he promised that the students would be limited to a penny per visit and seek out Sister Bradish only if they were sick or in "want of comfortable bread and beer in the college."

Wait, um, isn't that last condition the reason the students had been frequenting Bradish's Bread & Beer all along? Exactly. Even though Harvard had its own brewhouse and actually received payment in the form of barley and wheat from some students, the college had developed a reputation for skimping on rations. Defending Bradish, Dunster probably figured, "Why should I provide what this woman is already doing so well and for such a fair price?"

Some women also ran—and presumably brewed beer for—their own taverns. In an era when the untimely death of a spouse was a frequent woe, this was a common way for widows to support their families. A few women didn't even have to wait until they were widows. Take Dorothy "Goody" Upsall. She and her husband, Nicholas, were among the first settlers of Dorchester, Massachusetts, in 1630. An innkeeper since 1636, Nicholas got into trouble with the Puritan authorities for defending Quakers against persecution and/or for being a Quaker himself. He was jailed in the late 1650s and only allowed to return home if he kept a low profile. That's when Goody, beginning in 1659, "was allowed to draw beer" and, after Nicholas' death in 1666, "licensed to keep a public house of entertainment" until her own death in 1675. It's only a guess, but since the Upsall family was highly respected and the Puritans were to blame for Nicholas' diminished earning potential, they probably felt bad enough to let poor Goody support the family by selling beer. It was the least they could do.

A tavern was a pretty modest thing in those days. Running a "public house of entertainment" basically meant that you would open up your own home to travelers and others who would pay for a drink, a meal, and often a bed. Yet, taverns were more than that. For a group of people living on the edge of a vast, unexplored continent, they were little havens of civilization that provided a reliable supply of the universal beverage.

———◇———

The central role taverns played in early New England is well documented but not widely known. People think, "Hmm, Puritans...

weren't they strict zealots who hated fun?" Much of the time, yes. But even they needed a place outside of the home and the church—a place to conduct business and political affairs, to gossip about the neighbors, to swap farming tips. And those things were usually done, as was the English custom, before, during, or after a beer.

The Puritans depended on public houses like modern New Englanders depend on Dunkin' Donuts. There was at least one in every town, and towns were proliferating. Between 1629 and 1640 roughly twenty thousand people, mostly in families, left England to settle in the northern colonies and take part in the mission from God. (The promise of cheap land, economic opportunity, and just plain adventure sweetened the pot.) Groups of newcomers quickly fanned out and established new settlements in Massachusetts, Rhode Island, and Connecticut as well as southern New Hampshire and Maine.

When you're starting a new civilization, especially one that's supposed to impress the Creator, you have to rally the faithful not just religiously, but politically and socially. For our Yankee ancestors, the church took care of the former and the tavern helped with the latter. The tavern was a public institution, usually run by a respected man of the community, where civic business like court hearings and town planning was conducted, where social gatherings, business meetings, and military drills were held, and, of course, where travelers bunked and people drank. During the 1600s and 1700s, New England had more taverns than any other part of British North America.

One of the first things a town's settlers usually did was build a tavern, preferably right next to the church, or meetinghouse. Yes, especially on frigid winter Sundays, the congregation would file from the unheated meetinghouse to the tavern for a nip by the fireplace.

The Massachusetts Bay Colony General Court actually took some towns to task for failing to establish a public house. In 1660 it reprimanded Concord, Massachusetts, which was founded in the 1630s, for not having a "common house of entertainment," and threatened to fine the town if it didn't soon recruit an upstanding citizen to take on the role of tavern keeper. Concord promptly complied.

What *did* the people of Concord do for thirty years without a tavern? They probably just gathered at the houses of friends who brewed beer informally. Off-the-books brewing and tavernkeeping were prevalent enough that, as early as 1635, the General Court decreed that no one could run a tavern without a license. The product these rogue victualers were putting out must have offended some customers enough to prompt a 1651 law restricting brewing to those with "sufficyent skill and knowledge in the art or mistery of a brewer."

The Puritans were big on licensing and regulation. This wasn't necessarily because they wanted to limit the number of taverns, but rather

John Taylor, A Brown Dozen of Drunkards (1648).

to ensure that these prominent establishments were run by responsible people who sold decent drink at a fair price. They went so far as to specify what quantity of barley malt should be used, and what price should be charged, for different strengths of beer. And in 1649 they ordered every innkeeper to provide "good and wholesome beer, for the entertainment of strangers, who, for want thereof, are necessitated to too much needless expence in wine."

You'll be shocked, *shocked*, to know that some of these regulations backfired. Like the one in 1637 that ordered tavernkeepers to stop brewing themselves and instead purchase their beer from a licensed brewer. Problem was, they only licensed one brewer—the aforementioned Captain Sedgwick of Charlestown, who couldn't keep up with demand. So everybody drank more hard liquor instead. Oops.

—◇—

If you drink beer like water and, at the same time, consider drunkenness a sin, you're going to have a complicated relationship with alcohol. That was the Puritans' conundrum. Maybe John Winthrop should have campaigned harder for the benefits of drinking straight from New England's natural springs—for breakfast and lunch, at least. Beer may consist mostly of water, but, as we all know, it has enough alcohol in it to get a person drunk when over-consumed.

Drunkenness was a crime in early New England—the most common crime, actually. Lascivious behavior and Sabbath-breaking were not even close. Most offenders got off with a fine, but some were whipped, put in the stocks, or made to wear a badge of shame—just like the adulterers in *The Scarlet Letter*, only the drunkards wore a "D." And they didn't get a novel written about them.

Yet, the view that beer was innocent prevailed. If people could get decent, affordable beer, the thinking went, they'd steer clear of the hard stuff and would not get drunk. Alas, the Puritans' utopic vision of a temperate citizenry that went out for a couple of pints and returned home to read the Bible didn't pan out. For various reasons over the next century and a half, beer would be joined and even replaced by other alcoholic drinks, and drunkenness would reach new heights.

But beer would hold on and eventually survive. In a few eras, including today's, it would actually thrive. Like those hardy people who first landed at Plymouth and Boston, it turns out we really enjoy the stuff.

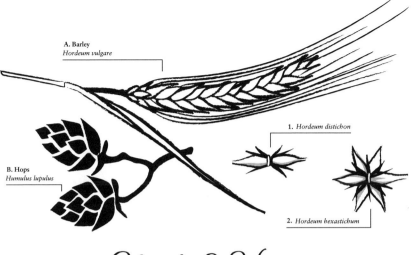

A. Barley
Hordeum vulgare

B. Hops
Humulus lupulus

1. *Hordeum distichon*

2. *Hordeum hexastichum*

Malt & Hops

What is beer? It's a beverage made from malted grain—primarily barley but also wheat, rye, corn, rice, oats, and other grains. Malting involves moistening grain until it begins to sprout and has produced all the starchy goodness necessary for the growth of the plant, then drying it and thus preserving it in its nutrient-rich state. Just crush the malt and add water, and you get a sugary liquid that yeast ferments into an alcoholic beverage. Mmm.

Walk into just about any craft brewery in New England, and there will be sacks of malted grain stacked in a pile. A lot of that malt comes from Canada. Some comes from Wisconsin, Great Britain, or Germany. None of it has come from New England—until very recently, that is.

In 2010, Andrea Stanley and her husband, Christian, were thinking of starting their own brewery near their farmstead in western

Massachusetts, a mecca for locally made beer. They envisioned people detouring off the nearby bike path and stopping by for a pint, preferably one brewed with locally produced malt. Andrea called the Paper City Brewery, a few miles down the road in Holyoke, to ask about suppliers of local malt. There was a pause as the brewer on the other end of the line puzzled over the question. Local malt? There was no such thing. People got their malt from agriculture giants like Cargill.

"I was intrigued," says Andrea. The Stanleys changed their business plan. They wouldn't be brewers; they'd be maltsters. Yes, maltsters—like Samuel Adams. That's right, New England's most famous patriot didn't actually make beer; he made *malt*.

That's how Valley Malt of Hadley, Massachusetts, began. The Stanleys knew that there was a market for their product. Small-scale brewers were locavores before "locavore" was even a word. These brewers pride themselves on the fact that they make beer to be consumed primarily within an hour's drive from where it's brewed, and using local ingredients is the logical next step for them. The Stanleys had also taken note of the exploding number of small breweries in the region.

But no one had made malt in New England since Prohibition. Andrea speculates that they faced challenges similar to those faced by the first craft brewers. Where would they

Failed maltster Samuel Adams.
Alonzo Chappel (1858).

procure raw materials and equipment? How would they acquire the know-how to make their product?

They joined a Google forum of people around the country and in Canada who were interested in malting. She and Christian read obscure, old farming texts and sought out experts on the agriculture of grain. Luckily, Christian's a mechanical engineer; he built the elevator-sized, stainless-steel malting vessels that squeeze into a well-ventilated garage on the Stanleys' property. Andrea found a few farmers in the area who were willing to cultivate barley fit for beer instead of cattle feed. In some cases, she has approached farmers with her own barley seed and asked them to grow it.

"Nobody has asked a farmer in New England to grow malting barley for decades," she says. The barley growers negotiated with Valley Malt on a fair pricing scheme for both parties. "They're kind of mentoring us."

The Stanleys are also getting some grain from Maine, New Hampshire, and Vermont and are growing forty acres of barley on their own land in Hadley. Being farmers in addition to maltsters, the Stanleys forged friendly relationships with grain experts like Harold Bockelman of the United States Department of Agriculture who helped Valley Malt get hold of the types of barley that were grown in New England from the 1600s through the early 1800s. These obscure varieties hold no value for agribusiness or megabrewers, but they're exactly the thing that craft brewers love—an ingredient that could lend unique characteristics and local terroir to beer.

Early adopters of Valley Malt in Massachusetts include the Wormtown Brewery of Worcester, the People's Pint in Greenfield, and the Cambridge Brewing Company in Cambridge, which began a "Valley Girl" series of specialty brews. Another early customer was the Throwback Brewery of North Hampton, New Hampshire. The brewer, Nicole Carrier, happens to be Andrea's cousin.

All told, Valley Malt has about fifty brewing and distilling customers, most of whom still depend on their regular suppliers for the majority of their grain. The Stanleys and their one part-time employee produce about ten tons of malt every week, which may sound like a lot until you realize that's only enough to wholly supply a handful of small breweries. Still, Valley Malt is turning a profit, and as it increasingly demonstrates that small-scale malting can succeed as a business—as others did with small-scale brewing thirty years ago—new entrepreneurs will join in, adding to New England's rich beer-making industry.

———◆———

As small as Valley Malt's operation is, New England's first settlers would have marveled at it—especially the magical part where you control the temperature and moisture of the malting vessels with a smart phone. There were no malthouses in the New World when the Europeans arrived, of course. They had to build their own. But first, they had to plant barley.

You can make beer out of just about any fermentable plant material. People have brewed beer out of corn, pumpkin, and molasses, to name just a few. Those ingredients are fine in a pinch, but if you want to brew beer of any quality, you must use barley.

For the seven-thousand-plus years that people have been brewing beer, barley has been the preferred grain. It was one of the first cereal crops cultivated by humans—most likely for the production of beer, as it doesn't make the greatest loaf of bread. Recipes etched on stone tablets and residue from clay pots in ancient Mesopotamia, Sumeria, and Egypt indicate that humankind's ancestors enjoyed barley beer.

Barley is ideal for brewing for two main reasons: it has a high percentage of starch, and it has special enzymes that break down that starch during the mashing process and convert it to fermentable sugar. What that means for the beer drinker is that, compared to other grains, barley produces a mellow and complex fresh-baked bread characteristic with a mild sweetness.

*Andrea and Christian Stanley, founders of Valley Malt
in Hadley, MA, courtesy of Andrea Stanley.*

Sounds nice, right? The English sure thought so, which is why they carried barley with them to plant in the colonies. The grain was probably first sown in 1602 on Martha's Vineyard and the Elizabeth Islands by Bartholomew Gosnold, the English explorer who named Cape Cod. It was one of the first things the Pilgrims planted when they came ashore in 1620. The harvest that they famously celebrated with the Wampanoags included barley, which we can wager they brewed into the first Thanksgiving ale. Farmers in the Massachusetts Bay Colony planted barley in Saugus in August 1632 and reported an exceptional harvest in Lynn in 1633.

Once the barley was growing, it had to be harvested and malted. The earliest New England malthouse was recorded in 1641. According to *A History of American Manufactures from 1608 to 1860* (1864), "John Appleton, one of the first settlers at Watertown, Massachusetts, who was frequently elected a representative to the General Court … received permission to set up a malt-house in that place. He is said also to have been a cultivator of hops. Samuel Livermore followed the same business there in 1667."

Records in Rhode Island, where barley was widely cultivated, show two maltsters, Matthew Greenell and Daniel Greenhill, operating in Portsmouth in 1681 and 1683, respectively. Yet records of commercial malting in this period are sparse. As *American Manufactures* notes, "Many years elapsed, in some parts of the country, before barley was raised in sufficient quantity for the production of malt and Beer, and a considerable importation of malt annually took place for the use of the brewers."

New England farmers did their best to grow barley. In the letters that John and Abigail Adams wrote to each other, the health of the barley crop at their Braintree, Massachusetts, farm comes up frequently. Writing to Abigail during his vice-presidency in 1794, John breaks the news that he won't be home until planting season is well underway. He then offers some affectionate words of support and advice to the woman who ran the farm while he was off running the country. "You are so valourous and noble a farmer that I feel little anxious about agriculture. Manure in hills, if you think best: but manure your barley ground well and harrow it well."

There were times when barley thrived in New England soil. Records show that Massachusetts farmers sent large amounts of the grain to New York in 1763, that the British stole bags of it during the siege of Boston in 1775, and that traders shipped it to Europe and the West Indies in the early 1800s. Some farms in Rhode Island and near the Connecticut coast were known for producing barley after the Revolution. Rhode Island, in fact, listed the grain as its leading agricultural product in 1796. "Exported, New England barley had a good reputation to the southward," writes Howard S. Russell in *A Long, Deep Furrow: Three Centuries of Farming in New England* (1982).

The Connecticut River Valley, with its rich soil, was New England's grain belt through much of the colonial era and beyond. In their effort to resurrect local malting barley, Andrea and Christian Stanley were inspired by records showing that there were malt houses in their region three hundred and fifty years ago. As late as 1872, the Connecticut River town of Walpole, New Hampshire, produced a bountiful thirty-three thousand bushels of barley.

For the most part, however, New England has never produced vast quantities of beer's staple grain. Of course, the region's six states are not vast themselves. New York and Pennsylvania, with farmland acreage that dwarfed New England's, were more suitable for cereal crops. The quantity of barley that grew in those states as their settlement progressed helped make them powerhouses of brewing.

"It was not until the closing decades of the eighteenth century, when settlement had pushed down the Mohawk Valley to western New York, that the widespread occurrence of ecologic conditions truly suited to the growing of high-quality barley was found in the eastern United States ... By 1820 two-thirds of the barley in the United States was being produced in New York," writes John Weaver in "Barley in the United States: A Historical Sketch," a journal article published in 1943. And when the Erie Canal opened in 1825, that barley could more easily be shipped far and wide.

Until then, New Englanders did one of two things when they couldn't grow their own: import or improvise.

———◇———

Coastal towns leaned toward the import strategy, as they had fairly easy access to malt shipped from Europe. But brewers living outside shipping centers had to get creative. Very creative. Not that they lacked the pluck and the know-how. "The settlers brought with them an English tradition of using substitute ingredients whenever necessary. Wheat or oats would certainly do if barley was lacking. But they also experimented with persimmons, pumpkins and the Jerusalem artichoke," writes Stanley Baron in *Brewed in America.*

If you think those ingredients sound weird, consider this stanza from "New England's Annoyances," a funny, tongue-in-cheek poem written anonymously in 1630:

> If barley be wanting to make into malt
> We must be content and think it no fault
> For we can make liquor to sweeten our lips
> Of pumpkins and parsnips and walnut-tree chips.

Possibly the first verse written by an American colonist, "New England Annoyances" shows not only the colonists' love of beer, but also that the essential Yankee character was already fully developed. It facetiously catalogs the brutal weather, the poor soil, the garden-munching varmints, and the monotonous diet of squash and root vegetables. But it ends on a sincere note, telling would-be New Englanders "to forsake not the honey for fear of the sting/but bring both a quiet and contented mind/and all needful blessings you surely will find." *Calling all quiet, resilient types: You're just going to love it here.*

When you consider how many settlers perished of starvation and disease in those early years, it's no wonder people resorted to pumpkin beer. To be clear, I'm talking about something far cruder than today's nutmeg-laced "pumpkin" ales that are made with little to no actual pumpkin. Here's a typical recipe, from a Virginia homebrewer in 1771, for "pompion" ale: "Let the pompion be beaten in a trough and pressed as apples. The expressed juice is to be boiled in a copper a considerable time and carefully skimmed that there may be no remains of the fibrous part of the pulp. After that intention is answered let the liquor be hopped cooled fermented etc. as malt beer." This sort of beverage is obscure for a reason.

Besides pumpkins, early New Englanders fashioned recipes from two other ingredients abundant in the colonies: corn and molasses. Corn had long been cultivated by the Indians and was so abundant a crop that figuring out how to brew a decent beer with it had been a logical pursuit almost since the first Europeans made landfall. The importance of the endeavor was such that John Winthrop Jr., governor of Connecticut and son of the Massachusetts governor, presented a paper on the "malting of maize" in 1662 to the leading scientific institution of the time, the Royal Society in London.

In his paper, Winthrop begins, "The English have found out a way to make very good beer of this grain which they do either out of bread made of it, or by malting of it." He goes on to describe each method, the second of which—malting the corn—is much more complex and time consuming than the first. Not surprisingly, he reports that since the simpler method of brewing with a crude version of cornbread results in a beer that is as "well colored, and pleasant, and every way as good and very wholesome without any windy quality, and keepeth better from souring than any other beer of that corn, therefore that way of brewing is most in use."

There are many other accounts of brewing from corn in colonial times, and they tend to go something like this: *We brewed an ale from maize! It tasted just as good as the stuff at home!* It's like the pleasant surprise young adults experience when cooking a meal in their first apartment. The very improbability of an edible dinner elevates its quality. *We made spaghetti tossed with chili powder and mayo—it was delicious!* Or at least without any "windy quality."

While brewing beer entirely out of corn is a suspect enterprise, brewing beer out of corn *and* barley is a long-established American tradition. After all, as colonists expanded west, so did corn. The grain belt of the Midwest emerged as a bountiful source of this and other cereal crops, including barley. When brewing became a large, competitive industry in that region in the 1800s, how could breweries resist adding corn—still easier to grow and cheaper than other grains—to their recipes in order to reduce production costs and increase profits? Plus, corn makes for a lighter-bodied beer, which was the direction the beverage took once lager dominated the market.

The legacy of these developments is that today's American mega-brewers use a large percentage of corn—as much as 40 percent—in their mass-market beers. Anheuser-Busch InBev uses another "adjunct" grain, rice, in the Budweiser product line. Craft brewers, who resurrected flavorful, all-barley beers in the 1980s, scorn the brewing-industrial complex's use of adjunct ingredients. Indeed, the Brewers Association, which advocates for craft brewers, defines craft beer as being "generally made with traditional ingredients like malted barley; interesting and sometimes non-traditional ingredients are often added for distinctiveness" rather than to lighten beer's flavor.

For our fore-Yankees, "non-traditional" beer ingredients were simply a fact of life. It seems when they weren't brewing beer with corn, they were brewing beer with molasses. Molasses and the beverage distilled from it, rum, were major trade commodities in the American colonies. Basically the muck left over from the production of cane sugar, molasses was shipped from the sugarcane plantations of the Caribbean to New England, where it was made into rum and used to flavor such Yankee delicacies as baked beans, brown bread, and molasses cookies.

The molasses supply, like the corn supply, was much more plentiful and reliable than the malted barley supply. That's how we got spruce beer, a popular style that was most often brewed in the home but sometimes commercially. It's called spruce beer because it's brewed with the tips of spruce tree branches in place of hops, but its base ingredient is molasses. When the Second Continental Congress met in Philadelphia shortly after the Battle of Lexington and Concord in 1775, George Washington, the newly appointed commander of the Continental Army, specified rations for his soldiers that included "1 quart of spruce beer or cyder per man per day."

New Englanders continued to brew molasses-based beers long after the Continental Army declared victory against the British. How-to books for farmers and homemakers from the early to mid-1800s, such as *The American Frugal Housewife* by Lydia Maria Child and *The New Eng-*

A modern spruce beer, courtesy of Harpoon Brewery.

land Farrier and Family Physician by Josiah Richardson, contain recipes for molasses brews. Some of these recipes were later revived in an odd little publication, *The Homemade Beer Book* (1973). This slim volume details the 1932 "proceedings" of the Company of Amateur Brewers, which is what a group of homebrewing enthusiasts in Vermont called themselves as they rode out the final years of Prohibition. One of the company's members, the guy who compiled the book, was Vrest Orton, who started the famous, old-timey Vermont Country Store and mail-order catalog.

Modern brewers have, from time to time, tried their hand at the weird, old beers of bygone New England. A few years back, Will Meyers of the Cambridge Brewing Company made a brew with molasses, some wild hops he found growing along the Minuteman Trail, and a type of amber malt that might have been found in a Revolutionary-era brewhouse. The finished product, he says slyly, "was lacking elegance, but it was interesting from a historical perspective."

More recently, Bill Goldfarb of Lefty's Brewing Company in Greenfield, Massachusetts, brewed a batch of spruce, molasses, and rye beer for the re-opening of the historic Deerfield Inn. And Butch Heilshorn and Alex McDonald of the Portsmouth, New Hampshire nanobrewery Earth Eagle Brewings made a sort of kitchen-sink colonial ale for the opening of a Strawbery Banke Museum exhibit on Portsmouth's brewing history. In addition to corn, molasses, and barley, they threw in wheat, oats, parsnips (just like in "New England's Annoyances"), and spruce tips. It tasted surprisingly like a traditional ale, only with a piney character instead of the usual hoppy one.

That craft brewers in the 2010s are willing to experiment with molasses is pretty ironic given that the authorities in early New England were as critical of this dreaded adjunct as today's craft brewers are of corn and rice. As early as 1667, Puritan lawmakers tried to ban molasses in brewing. "The issue of quality prompted Massachusetts to legislate beer regulations stipulating that beer had to be made from good quality malt and could not be diluted with molasses or coarse sugar," writes Gregg Smith in *Beer in America: The Early Years—1587-1840* (1998). There were also occasional bans on imports of European barley malt in order to stimulate domestic malt production so that the use of adjuncts could be avoided in the first place. But the local barley malt supply would simply never catch up with the locals' demand for beer. The local hops supply, meanwhile, fared a little better.

———◆———

Hops grow on vines and look like delicate little green pine cones about the size of the pad of a man's thumb. They contain acids and essential oils that add bitterness, flavor, and aroma to beer and act as a natural preservative. Malt is the basic raw material of beer; hops are the spice. Most of the time, they are dried, crushed, and formed into little pellets like rabbit food that are easier to transport, store, and work with than what are called whole flowers.

Ever wondered about the difference between beer and ale? It

used to hinge on hops. English ale underwent a transformation when Dutch brewers introduced hops to England in the 1400s. For a while, "beer," as the Dutch called their malt beverage, was the stuff that contained those bitter foreign plants. Unhopped "ale" was the traditional, native malt beverage. "The original English ale has been described as sweetish—stronger and more perishable than hopped beer," writes Baron.

The English eventually realized that hops lent a pleasant balance to the malty sweetness of ale and slowed its spoilage. By the time they started to colonize the New World, ale was a hopped beverage, and so began centuries of confusion about the difference between ale and beer. A 1692 English brewing manual, *Cerevisiarii Comes: Or the New and True Art of Brewing*, uses the terms interchangeably. But a distinction between the two lingered. In 1797, Samuel Deane, a vice president of Maine's Bowdoin College, published a reference work called *The New England Farmer* that includes an entry on beer and brewing. It begins, "Beer, a pleasant drink made with malt and hops … is distinguished from ale by having a greater quantity of hops; whence it is more bitter, and will keep longer." These days the primary categories are ale and lager, and we differentiate them by the type of yeast that ferments them.

Hops aren't that difficult to grow in New England. Get a hop root, stick it in the dirt, make sure it has a pole or string to climb, and watch the vine twirl upwards and come back each year bearing plump cones in late summer. When our fore-Yankees arrived on these shores, they found hops growing wild in the forest, and they happily put them to use in brewing. Soon, however, as with barley, they began to cultivate hops in response to steady demand for the universal beverage.

The Massachusetts Bay colonists, as usual, weren't taking any chances when it came to hitting the ground brewing. In addition to an ample supply of beer and malt, they shipped over from England four hundred pounds of hops in 1628. That was the beginning of an eventual golden age of hop cultivation in New England. From the mid-1700s until the 1830s, Massachusetts was the leader in hop production in North America. Middlesex County was known in particular for the crop. Records from the 1700s show Massachusetts hops being exported to Virginia, New York, and Newfoundland.

Woburn may have been the first New England town known for hop production. In 1702, Judge Samuel Sewall, who presided over the Salem witch trials and wrote diaries about his travels in the Bay Colony, mentions a visit to a Woburn hop yard. Neighboring towns followed in Woburn's footsteps, particularly Wilmington, which at one point was known as Hop Town.

By the late 1700s, Massachusetts was exporting a considerable amount of hops to France and Germany. In 1802, the colony instituted the inspection and grading of all hops, which established a high standard. This "so impressed European buyers that they regularly requested the 'first sort' Massachusetts variety," writes Michael Tomlan in *Tinged with Gold: Hop Culture in the United States* (1992). "This, in turn, allowed the sellers to charge a higher price ... Glowing reports of enormous profits were common, and production spread beyond Massachusetts to New Hampshire, Maine, and Vermont."

A Wilmington farmer named William Campbell moved to Bedford, in Hillsborough County, New Hampshire, around 1800 and brought some hop roots with him. Within a few decades, the county became a signifi-

A man and his malt. Bill Goldfarb at Lefty's Brewing Company, courtesy of Melissa Forostoski.

cant producer of the crop, even taking the lead among all U.S. counties in 1840. Maine hops were primarily grown in the Oxford County towns of Brownfield, Buckfield, Denmark, Dixfield, and Hiram, and were shipped domestically and abroad via Portland.

Vermont also enjoyed a hop heyday beginning in the 1840s. Just as a few Wilmington, Massachusetts, farmers migrated to Bedford, New Hampshire, to spread hops around, some of Bedford's citizens in turn moved to Bethel, Vermont, with hop roots in their pockets around 1825. By 1850, Vermont was producing 8 percent of the national crop (second to New York), and ten years later it tripled its output as every county in the state got in on the action.

If it sounds like New England was once showered in hops, it wasn't. Maybe most of the crop was going abroad to the highest bidders. After all, there was really only one large-scale brewery in New England, the Boston Beer Company, before 1850. In any case, plenty of people in New England—homebrewers, small commercial brewers, tavern keepers—lacked access to hops. The prevalence of spruce beer is proof of this predicament.

After the Civil War, the New England hops boom ended. Prices for the crop are notoriously volatile to begin with, and the wild swings in the region's weather—too cold, too wet, too hot, too dry—made hops susceptible to blight and rot. Plus, like barley, the crop was inexorably heading west. New York had already taken over as the nation's hop capital by the 1840s. But wait … wasn't it two Massachusetts natives, James Cooledge and Solomon Root, who first grew hops commercially in the Empire State in the early 1800s? Yup.

And get this: the vaunted hop culture of the Pacific Northwest, by far the dominant growing region in today's United States, has New England origins. In the 1850s, Daniel and Wilson Flint, brothers who grew up on a farm in Swanzey, New Hampshire, brought Vermont hops with them to the San Francisco Bay area. Their growing experiments were successful enough that Daniel bought some farmland in Sacramento and transported the plants there. So began the first known hopyard on the West Coast, as well as the first hop kiln and hop press. Daniel had discovered that the crop grew almost magically in the northern California climate.

"The mind of an Eastern hop grower, where it takes three years from the planting to get a full crop and then only from five to eight hundred pounds to the acre, is hardly prepared to comprehend that we grow two thousand pounds to the acre the first year the roots are planted," he wrote.

The trouble was he could barely get California brewers to notice their native bounty. They got their hops from the East—who didn't?— and swore by them. Flint finally convinced a prominent brewer to try the local hops and, if he didn't like them, he wouldn't have to pay for them. The brewer liked them. Very much. He ended up buying Flint's entire crop. Eventually, writes Tomlan, "brewers of San Francisco and Sacramento gradually came to realize that the California hop easily rivaled the eastern product in freshness and quality, and local hop growers began to prosper. The demand for roots increased, so that prominent growers, such as Daniel Flint, soon reported the sale of thousands of dollars of cuttings from their yards."

Many of those cuttings made their way north to Oregon and Washington, completing the West Coast's fertile hop belt. Flint later wrote that "the three Pacific States have soil and climate to furnish hops for the world"—thanks to the New Hampshire farm boy who put them on the map.

The world of hops is so West Coast-centric these days, it's hard to imagine that California brewers once scoffed at the notion that good hops could be grown in their backyard. A lot of Eastern craft brewers are inspired by the creativity and boldness of their counterparts in the West, where the American craft-beer revolution began. It seems like a new hop variety comes out of the Pacific Northwest every day, giving birth to a dozen new hoppy beers.

Well, guess what? The East Coast is looking to rejoin the party. Over the past decade, small farmers in New York have begun to revive that state's once-dominant hop industry, and now New Englanders are poised to put their own hops back on the map. Just as Valley Malt has answered brewers' demand for locally produced malt, hop farmers have recently emerged around New England to see if supplying hops might once again be a viable business.

So far, Maine boasts the greatest number of commercial hop growers (and the quaintest farm names): Duck Trap River Hop Farm in Lincolnville, Rock Island Hop Farm in Sanford, and a cooperative in Monroe made up of Irish Hill Farm, Elm Hill Farm, and Marsh Stream Hops. These south and mid-coast growers are joined by two northern ones: Aroostook Hops in Westfield and the Hop Yard in Fort Fairfield (the Hop Yard also has a field in Gorham). Collectively, these suppliers have provided local flavor to Maine craft breweries including Allagash, Black Bear, Gritty McDuff's, and Sebago.

Ocean State Hops in Exeter, Rhode Island, established its hopyard in 2007. The Newport Storm brewery uses the farm's spicy Chinook hops to dry-hop its India Point Ale. (Dry-hopping involves steeping an extra dose of hops in beer during the conditioning stage in order to maximize the ingredient's aromas and flavors.)

On the research and development side, there's the Vermont Hops Project at the University of Vermont Extension in St. Albans, which began in 2010. Heather Darby, a young agronomist and Vermont native, leads a team of soil and crop experts in an effort to determine which hop varieties will best thrive in New England and helps farmers with cultivation and harvesting practices. Connecticut's department of agriculture and the University of Southern Connecticut have also undertaken a study on the feasibility of growing hops locally.

It's all very experimental at the moment. Most, if not all, hop growers in New England still have day jobs. Their small farms are never going to compete on the level of the behemoth industry out west. But that's not their goal. If they can grab a chunk of the Northeast's booming craft-brewing market, with its increasing clamor for local ingredients, they'll probably consider themselves successful. But first, like any start-up industry, they have to overcome challenges of infrastructure and labor. The trellis systems upon which hop vines climb are a considerable investment, and no small grower can afford harvesting equipment. That translates into hours of human labor, as each little hop cone must be plucked off the vine by hand.

Modern hop farmers face the same challenges as our Yankee ancestors did when it came to making their beloved beverage. Hops grow well in New England and, contrary to what many believe, barley doesn't do too poorly either. However, in both colonial and modern times, there has been little to no infrastructure or extra labor to produce beer's raw materials on a large scale. In the region's early history, much of the population was essentially camping as people rapidly branched out from established communities to found new ones. Who had the wherewithal to build a commercial malt house or pick an acre of hops? And by the time anybody did have the wherewithal, hard liquor had dug in; it was so portable!

It's a testament to the human thirst for malt beverages that they survived the American pre-Industrial period at all. Especially because there was another drink that competed with beer. Early New Englanders found that the fruit trees they brought over from the Old World took to their new home's climate and soil beautifully. Soon, branches were dripping with apples and pears. People said, "Screw malting barley and picking hops. Let's crush fruit and drink cider." And who could blame them? Despite this, beer hung on—in taverns, on the battlefield, on merchant ships—and emerged triumphant during the Industrial Age.

Barrels

In the modern American beer industry, a barrel is not so much a container as it is a unit of measure. One barrel equals thirty-one gallons. (A standard keg is known as a half-barrel, or fifteen and one half gallons.) The largest craft brewery in New England, Boston-based Harpoon[1], produces two hundred thousand barrels of beer per year. The largest brewery in New England, Anheuser-Busch's plant in Merrimack, New Hampshire, produces just over three million—a fraction of the almost ninety-nine million barrels the company brews annually in the United States.

Almost all of these "barrels" of beer are dispensed from kegs, bottles, or cans. The wooden cask we think of when we picture a barrel

[1] You might ask, "Isn't the Boston Beer Company, maker of Samuel Adams, the largest brewery in New England?" No. The Boston-based company brews all but a small portion of its beer outside New England.

became obsolete in the beer industry after Prohibition—well, almost. Many craft brewers age some of their beer in casks that have been recycled from bourbon distilleries, wineries and sherry or port producers. They do this not because they've run out of kegs but to lend interesting flavors to their brews. A barrel may be a specialty item today, but during the 2,000-odd years between its invention and the advent of modern packaging, it was *the* container for beer.

It was the container for almost everything, actually. Flour and fish, tar and tobacco, maize and madeira. When barrels were the universal container, making them—being a cooper—was a common profession. The most skilled coopers were those who made leak-proof casks that held liquids.

Probably the best-known cooper in American history was John Alden, *Mayflower*-passenger-turned-literary figure who wooed Priscilla away from rival Miles Standish. Did you know that this hunky craftsman only accompanied the Pilgrims to Plymouth as a hired hand to

Modern beer barrels, courtesy of Allagash Brewery.

mind their barrels of ale during the ocean crossing? Luckily for American history and Henry Wadsworth Longfellow's writing career, he decided to stick around.

Made of curved wood staves arranged in a bulging cylinder and bound with hoops of wood or iron, barrels were sturdy and could be easily rolled and spun when placed on their sides. Their portability was key. As much as early New Englanders needed raw materials to brew beer, they needed barrels for storage and distribution.

The story of barrels is the story of beer on the move—beer on ships and on the battlefield, beer in the tavern, beer spilling into historical events. It is also the story of beer on the run from other liquids, especially cider and rum, which seriously challenged its position as the universal beverage in pre-Industrial New England.

———◇———

Beer was closely linked to New England's shipping industry, which rose in prominence within decades of the first settlements. More so than the middle and southern colonies, the northern ones excelled in this endeavor. They had to. As the historian Malcolm Keir explains, "Although all the thirteen colonies had access to the sea, in none of them was the influence of tidewater so potent as in the New England settlements. Since the Middle and Southern colonies were better endowed with agricultural wealth than New England, tillage of the soil was their foremost activity. New England alone, poor in farm produce, turned from the niggardly soil to the generous ocean, where fishing and commerce became the sources of her greatness and gave rise to almost all of her other activities."

New Englanders built their own ships, too; there was a continent full of timber in their backyard. In 1700, Boston was the third-largest shipping port in the entire British Empire, behind only London and Bristol.

All of these boats needed beer. It was as much a staple at sea as on land, and for the same reason: water's bad reputation. Ships did carry water for drinking and cooking, but as it sat warm for weeks in wooden barrels, it grew foul with algae and bacteria. Alcohol kept those at bay, so mariners preferred to wash down their hardtack with beer. They were also under the impression that beer could prevent scurvy—the sailor's scourge—with its dreaded symptoms of bleeding gums and festering wounds. Luckily, they would eventually discover the actual antiscorbutic power of citrus fruits.

In the 1730s, Sampson Salter's brewery on Leverett's Lane in Boston (where Government Center now sits) supplied beer for ships outfitted by Peter Faneuil. The son of a French Huguenot who migrated to the American colonies, Faneuil was such a successful merchant that he built for his city the eponymous hall New Englanders recognize from walking the Freedom Trail and shopping at Quincy Market. Everyone from Samuel Adams and George Washington to Ted Kennedy and Bill Clinton has made historic appearances there.

Having clients like Faneuil helped make Salter one of the most successful commercial brewers in New England before the Revolution.

Peter Faneuil, eighteenth century portrait and Faneuil Hall circa 1740, courtesy of the National Archives.

He had a long career. His name appears in a letter written on his behalf by a business associate in 1766, when Salter was seventy-four. The letter demands that a New York customer of Salter's either send his empty beer barrel back to Boston or pay for the barrel if he intended to keep it. When you consider that Salter must have distributed thousands of barrels of beer during his brewing career, this says a lot about either his tenacity and frugality as a businessman or about the value of a barrel—or both.

Another Boston brewer named Robert Whatley also supplied merchant ships, notably those of Thomas Hancock, whose nephew John would inherit and expand his uncle's business before he helped start the American Revolution.

Newport, Rhode Island, whose overseas trade nearly rivaled that of Boston, had a notable brewer named Giles Hosier. In 1770, Giles and his partner, Thomas Robinson, a prominent local merchant, were looking for some cellar space to store their beer. They thought the basement of the Colony House (later the State House) was just the place. In a petition to rent the space, they wrote that it "has for a long time ben and now is unimproved and bringeth no profit to the Colony when at the same time it may be Rendered Serviceable to your Petitioners and of publick Utility." *Hey, if you legislators aren't doing anything with that basement, can we at least store our beer there?*

If sailors couldn't live without their beer ration, neither could soldiers. Official rations for the Continental Army included one quart of spruce beer or cider per man per day. Because beer's traditional ingredients, malt and hops, were often hard to come by in the colonies—especially during war—people improvised. If you'll recall, spruce beer was a common drink made with widely available molasses instead of malt and the tips of spruce branches instead of hops.

If a soldier's rations never showed up and/or he simply wanted more to drink, the sutler would come to the rescue. Sutlers ran little bodegas on the battlefield. They sold beer, liquor, and tobacco as well as cloth, sugar, razor blades, and other basics. A New Hampshire man named James Walker was a sutler during the French and Indian War. Walker's family, from northern Ireland, was among the first to settle the town of Bedford, Massachusetts in the 1730s. His father ran an inn, and thus the younger Walker would have been familiar with the tricks of the service trade. So, he picked up and made for upstate New York in 1760, supplying British troops at Fort Ticonderoga with sugar, cheese, tobacco, chocolate, and soap along with barrels of spruce beer and rum. Seventeen years later, he was fighting against those troops as a soldier at the Revolutionary War battle of Bennington, Vermont.

—◇—

The Green Dragon Tavern near Faneuil Hall in Boston is part of a conglomerate of Irish pubs. It serves "Patriot's Pleasures" such as Redcoat Wings and Loaded Musket Potato Skins and features live bands and comedians. It opened in 1993, although the pub's literature says that it was established in 1654.

Huh?

Actually, the current Green Dragon capitalizes on—oops, I mean, pays homage to—a historic tavern that was once located nearby. It was definitely not Irish. It was where, in the 1760s, a bunch of disgruntled British colonials started meeting regularly over beers to plot resistance to a severe bout of taxation without representation. Senator and statesman Daniel Webster later called it "the headquarters of the Revolution."

England, heavily in debt and seeking new revenue after the Seven Years' War (the French and Indian War to us), enacted a series of taxes and other measures that, in addition to being burdensome, ran roughshod over a long-established tradition of colonial self-government. It wasn't just economic hardship that angered the Yanks, it was the Crown's treatment of them as second-class British citizens; they had no representation in parliament, so they had no say in any of the

Green Dragon Tavern, courtesy of the Boston Public Library.

laws imposed on them. They wanted to be *first-class* British citizens. Not a chance, they were told.

That really pissed off Samuel Adams, who was agitating for independence from Britain. He and his fellow Sons of Liberty, including John Hancock, Paul Revere, and Joseph Warren, often hung out at the Green Dragon. Sometimes Adams' cousin John, straight-laced but sympathetic to the cause, would come along. Hancock, one of those affable rich guys who liked to hang out with radicals, often put a barrel of ale on his tab for the fellas. The merchant ships he inherited from his Uncle Thomas were, after all, targets of British customs agents.

Some of the talking points that Samuel Adams issued to win folks over to the "Sticking It to England" agenda had a "Made in America" theme. In one, he entreated brewers to help colonials forsake imported beer or spirits: "It is to be hoped, that the Gentlemen of the Town will endeavour to bring our own October Beer [strong beer] into Fashion again … so that we may no longer be beholden to Foreigners for a Credible Liquor, which may be as successfully manufactured in this Country."

Adams probably wouldn't have been pleased if any of the gentlemen of the town pointed out that he played a small part in contributing to the import problem by abandoning his father's malting business to become a politician.

In December 1773, with Adams leading the plot and Hancock supplying the liquid courage, a few dozen compatriots gathered at the Green Dragon to embark on the mission of sneaking aboard a ship in Boston Harbor and dumping several barrels of tea overboard in protest. The Boston radicals had graduated from boycotting British imports to destroying them. England responded in kind by closing the port of Boston and shutting down the provincial government.

You'd think that, after the Boston Tea Party, British soldiers occupying a rebellious city would avoid hanging out at patriot-dominated taverns—or that they would at least keep their voices down. But no. It's like when a pack of New York Yankees fans walks into Fenway Park and starts trashing the Red Sox pitching lineup. Not smart. Redcoats still brazen enough to frequent the Green Dragon didn't know, apparently, that the Sons of Liberty had spies all over the place keeping an ear out for conversation like, "Hey, did you know that we're marching into Concord tomorrow to seize the militia's guns and ammo?"

On the night of April 18, 1775, that bit of actionable intelligence was passed on to Revere, who quickly dispatched dozens of men, including himself, to ride out into the countryside to give everyone the heads-up. When the militiamen of Lexington, en route to Concord, got the news, they readied themselves for action by assembling at Buckman Tavern on the town green early the next morning. A customary recruiting tool for these volunteer militias, which made up a sizable portion of the Continental forces, was free beer at the local inn after practice drills.

This particular night was no practice drill. As roughly seven hundred British troops approached, a mere seventy-seven militiamen lined up on the green. No one knows who fired the first shot, but within minutes, eight militiamen had been gunned down and one British soldier was wounded. The war for independence had finally begun. Buckman Tavern served as a makeshift hospital for the wounded in the Battle of Lexington and Concord and no doubt consoled the survivors with something to drink.

When it wasn't being fought on battlefields, the American Revolution played out in taverns. These central public institutions were not only where the Sons of Liberty fomented rebellion, but also where members of the Continental Congress in Philadelphia hammered out details of the Declaration of Independence and where military commanders spent the night as they traveled from one battlefield to the next. "George Washington slept here" is one of the earliest American tourism slogans, found on little plaques in colonial-era buildings listed in the National Register of Historic Places. When Washington slept in those places, they were taverns.

Public houses all over New England became minor legends during the war. Take Alice Greele's in Portland, Maine, which the widow ran for thirty years beginning in the late 1750s. By the time of the Revolution, Portland (then called Falmouth Neck) had established its footing as a port town after tumultuous decades in which Maine was a battleground between England, France, and the Indians. Still part of the Massachusetts Bay Colony, Maine had its share of patriots who caused trouble for the British military, and Greele's was one of the places they frequented. The widow herself had notable patriotic spunk, according to the historian Nathan Goold writing in 1896:

"Alice Greele saved her house during [Britain's naval bombardment of Portland in 1775], by remaining in it and extinguishing the flames when it caught fire. It is said that a hot shot landed in her back yard and fired the chips. She took it up in a pan and threw it into the lane and said to a man, then passing, 'They will have to stop firing soon, for they have got out of bombs and are making new balls and can't wait for them to cool.'" The attack on Portland spurred the Second Continental Congress to hurry its plans for establishing a Continental Navy.

Vermont, another New England outpost emerging from decades as an embattled frontier, had Stephen Fay's Tavern in Bennington. Fay's became a hangout for Revolutionary War hero Ethan Allen and his fellow hard-drinking members of a brash local militia known as the Green Mountain Boys. Allen planned his daring raid on the British-held Fort Ticonderoga at Fay's Tavern in 1775, and New Hampshire's General John Stark stopped there while planning what would be the victorious Battle of Bennington in 1777.

The Green Mountain Boys got their start by defending the property rights of settlers who had land grants from New Hampshire. This soil was in a tug of war between New Hampshire and New York before Vermont became a state in 1791. At one point, the Boys shamed a "Yorker" sympathizer by tying him to a chair and hoisting him up the tavern's signpost. They had already crowned the signpost with a snarling, stuffed catamount pointed west, to send the Yorkers a message—hence Fay's popular nickname, the Catamount Tavern.

Tavern owners were in most cases prominent citizens who often participated in local government. One of Vermont's better-known

Drawing of the Catamount Tavern from Griswold Postcards, early 1900s.

innkeepers was its first governor, Thomas Chittenden. He played a leading role in establishing Vermont as an independent republic and in getting the green light from the Continental Congress to join the federal Union as the fourteenth state. The first settler of the town of Williston, just outside Burlington, Chittenden ran an inn for travelers who passed his farm on the Winooski River.

Another prominent New Englander who made a go at innkeeping was Israel Putnam, a hero in the French and Indian War who went on to greater fame as a general who led the valiant Yankees in the Battle of Bunker Hill. He named his inn in Brooklyn, Connecticut, the General Wolfe Tavern after the British officer who captured Quebec from the French in 1759. The tavern's weather-beaten sign, with its painted figure of General Wolfe gesturing gallantly, is now part of the Connecticut Historical Society's excellent exhibit of old New England tavern signs. Putnam ran his house of public entertainment from 1768 until 1775, when he dashed off to fight for the patriot cause upon hearing of Lexington and Concord.

One historian suggests that the General Wolfe Tavern was a thrifty Yankee's solution to the high cost of entertaining. Already a popular figure because of his bravery against the French and Indians, Putnam married a socially connected woman, and the couple began to get a lot of visitors. Ellen D. Larned laid out the situation in her 1880 history of Windham County:

> Relatives, friends, traveling ministers, distinguished strangers and gushing patriots came in such numbers that their entertainment became very burdensome. A Virginian Jefferson would submit to such an invasion though it made him bankrupt; a Yankee Putnam could contrive to turn it into profit, or at least save himself from ruin. Finding that his estate could not support such an excessive outlay, Putnam met the emergency with one of his sudden strokes, removed his residence to the Avery estate on Brooklyn Green, and opened his house

for general public accommodation ... That Brooklyn tavern, with Putnam for its landlord and Mrs. Avery Gardiner Putnam as mistress, became one of the most noted gathering places in Eastern Connecticut, and witnessed many a thrilling scene of the great Revolutionary drama.

—◇—

In a ledger from the Catamount Tavern that has been preserved by the Bennington Museum, customers' tabs list wine, rum, and toddy (a hot mixture of rum or other spirit, sugar, and water). Other common tavern drinks of the 1700s included punch (rum with citrus, tea, sugar, and water) and cider—yes, the hard kind. We can assume that many taverners were still brewing beer at this point, but the universal beverage of the 1630s had become merely one of a smorgasbord of alcoholic potions available. Wine competed with beer among the well off, but rum and cider were ubiquitous, especially in New England.

"If the ancients drank wine as our people drink rum and cider, it is no wonder we read of so many possessed with devils," John Adams famously mused after describing a drunken binge by one of his farmhands.

It is no surprise that rum took this new country hostage. Merchants often distilled rum right on the wharves of coastal New England as molasses from the West Indies poured off of ships. By 1750, there were an estimated thirty-five distilleries in Massachusetts, twenty in Rhode Island, five in Connecticut, and three in New Hampshire. High-quality Medford Rum, named for the Massachusetts town where it was produced, stood out among the mostly rotgut offerings of the period. Everyone drank rum. It was New England's top tipple for more than a century.

Rum introduced a cheap high to the masses. The average Josiah could get as inebriated as the prosperous merchant with his fancy-pants European brandy. The affluent, too, drank plenty of rum, only they got the good stuff made in the West Indies or Medford. As in substance-abuse epidemics throughout the history of humankind, the authorities were not so concerned with rich folk's overindulgence. In 1686, the Puritan minister Increase Mather delivered a sermon in which he remarked, "It is an unhappy thing that in later years a kind of strong Drink called Rum has been common amongst us, which the poorer sort of People, both in Town and Country, can make themselves drunk with … I wish to the Lord some Remedy may be thought of for the prevention of this evil."

Actually, there was a remedy: cider. Along with its alcoholically gentle siblings, beer and wine, it is the sort of thing Mather was talking about when, years before that rum-bashing sermon, he called drink "a good creature of god." Early temperance reformers, too, were A-OK with fermented beverages like cider. The Reverend Jeremy Belknap, New Hampshire's first historian, wrote in 1812, "The juice of the apple, the fermentation of barley, and the decoction of spruce are amply sufficient for the refreshment of man."

Whether cider was consumed instead of or alongside spirits, it was a popular drink. By the early 1700s, it had eclipsed beer as New Englanders' everyday beverage because apples were so much easier to grow, harvest, and ferment than barley and hops.

Reverend William Blackstone, the lone settler on the Shawmut Peninsula when the Puritans arrived and named it Boston, planted New England's first apple orchard on Beacon Hill in 1623. In 1634, he moved to Cumberland, Rhode Island, and planted his Yellow Sweetings apples there. Like Blackstone, New England's early settlers planted fruit trees as soon as they arrived. The Roxbury Russet, prized for cider and its ability to keep all winter, originated around 1647 in the Boston neighborhood for which it's named. Unlike most crops, apples thrived in New England's rocky soil. When the British officer Lord Adam Gordon traveled through New England in 1765, he wrote in his journal, "I never Saw such Quantities of Apple and Pear Trees, all the Roads are lined with them, the poorest Farmer … has one or more Orchards, and Cyder is their common Drink."

Yes, even the poorest farmer drank cider, and plenty of it. In 1764, Middlesex County in Massachusetts produced more than 33,400 barrels of cider, which works out to more than a barrel for every man, woman, and child. In the fairly typical case of one Andover, New Hampshire family of four, thirty barrels of cider in the cellar wasn't enough to get them through to the next harvest; they had to buy extra supplies. The distribution of cider was so important that it influenced infrastructure. When the people of Lancaster, Massachusetts agreed to build a road around Wachusett Mountain, they stipulated that it must be wide enough to "carry comfortably with four oxen, four barrels of cider, at once."

One of New England's most illustrious fans of cider was none other than John Adams, who seemed to throw the beverage under the bus alongside rum when railing against the alcoholism of colonial Americans. Actually, the second president of the United States considered cider on its own to be not only innocent but also essential. He grew his own cider apples and downed a glass every morning before breakfast.

Some New England cidermakers established a reputation for their product beyond their own pastures. The eccentric Shaker community of Canterbury, New Hampshire, for example, made such high-quality cider that it sold in Boston for as much as ten dollars a barrel—several times the price of inferior swill.

Beginning in the mid-1800s, cider died a gradual death. Temperance reformers chopped down entire orchards. The population shifted to urban areas, where German and Irish immigrants preferred beer or whiskey. Any old-timers still selling cider in 1919 were shut down by Prohibition. If someone wanted to revive the industry after Repeal, they were out of luck. New England's remaining few cider trees were finally finished off by twin disasters: the severe winter of 1934 and the Hurricane of '38.

Over the past few decades, hard cider has reemerged alongside

Testing barrels at Farnum Hill Cider in Lebanon, NH,
courtesy of Brenda Bailey Collins, Farnum Hill Ciders.

lost beer styles such as pale ale and porter. Most of that cider aspires
to be nothing more than a sweet alternative to mass-produced beer,
with a similar level of alcohol, carbonation, and flavor consistency.
But some small producers are making a more traditional version of
the beverage—relatively dry, complex and, like vintage wine, influenced by terroir and annual variations in the fruit harvest.

The rebirth of artisanal cider in New England and beyond owes
a lot to Steve Wood, who grows apples at Poverty Lane Orchards in
Lebanon, New Hampshire, and sells his cider under the label Farnum Hill. In a wild gamble, he began growing cider apples on his
farm in the 1980s and fermenting them into a beverage that no one
had demanded for one hundred years. By trial and error, he blended
fermentations from different apple varieties—English types such as

Ashmead's Kernel and Kingston Black, among others—until he began to create ciders with a richness and refined sharpness that beverage critics now consider benchmarks.

Crucially, Wood also gave cuttings of his trees to anyone who was willing to stick them in the ground and watch them grow. By both providing the raw materials and demonstrating what could be done with them, he helped create a market for traditional cider that is now being propelled forward by the demand for artisanal, local (and, to some extent, gluten-free) foods. New England now has a slew of cider makers, including West County Cider Winery in the Berkshires—which, like Farnum Hill, began in the 1980s—as well as newer start-ups such as Bantam and Downeast. Cider still falls far short of reclaiming its past dominance over beer, but Farnum Hill and others have at least made it cool again to drink like a Yankee farmer.

———◆———

Cider was often used as the basis of bygone tavern cocktails like sillabub and stone-fence or stone-wall. The former is a dessert-like mixture of cider, sugar, nutmeg, and cream. The latter is a stiff cocktail of cider and rum that fortified the likes of Ethan Allen and the Green Mountain Boys when they nabbed Fort Ticonderoga. The popularity of these cocktails—not to mention their wacky names—is proof that our predecessors weren't unfamiliar with a good time.

Other colonial cocktails used beer as their base, and this helped keep malt beverages alive during New England's long rum-and-cider phase. The undisputed king of these cocktails was flip. The colonists were mad for it, and the richest references to the beverage come from New England tavern records and historians. Worcester, Massachusetts native Alice Morse Earle's description of flip in her 1900 history, *Stage-coach and Tavern Days*, is often cited:

"Flip was made in a great pewter mug or earthen pitcher filled two-thirds full of strong beer; sweetened with sugar, molasses, or dried pumpkin, according to individual taste or capabilities; and flavored with a 'dash'—about a gill [5 ounces]—of New England rum. Into this mixture was thrust and stirred a red-hot loggerhead, made of iron and shaped like a poker, and the seething iron made the liquor foam and bubble ... and gave it the burnt, bitter taste so dearly loved."

Any innkeeper worth his salt kept a pitcher, flip glasses, and a hot poker handy for those who disembarked from the next stagecoach that pulled up at the door. If there was the slightest nip in the air, travelers would demand flip. Danforth's tavern in Cambridge, Massachusetts, Tilton's in Portsmouth, New Hampshire, Bowen's in Barrington, Rhode Island, and Dutton House in Cavendish, Vermont, are just a few examples of public houses that regularly served flip. Dutton House actually had on its sign an image of the dame of the house presenting a mug of flip to a thirsty traveller.

The Massachusetts towns of Canton and Holden were favored stops along the major stagecoach routes in the era before highways and railroads. That popularity had something to do with the quality of the flip at those towns' taverns. In Canton (home of today's Blue Hill Brewery), May's Tavern was a convenient stopping place for travelers headed north to Boston. Its "flip was delicious," according to a history of that town. The secret was the addition of a mixture of sugar, eggs, and cream that had been "thoroughly mixed and allowed to stand two days." Two days? No wonder they put so much rum in the drink.

Abbot's Tavern in Holden, on the route between Keene, New Hampshire, and Worcester, Massachusetts, also embellished its flip with eggs and cream. Beginning in 1763, three generations of Abbots ran the place for over one hundred years. Writing in 1894, one historian reports, "There are still many who remember the peculiar flavor of the beer which [Major Chenery Abbot] brewed and the rare quality of the flip which he prepared in a way of his own." The writer goes on to claim, "It is no exaggeration to state that Abbott's Hotel was known from the Pacific to the Atlantic Ocean."

That's quite a statement, but if there's any truth to it, I want to travel back in time and go to Abbot's with Alice Morse Earle. Pretty much any history of alcoholic beverages or drinking habits written in the last hundred years has referenced her *Stage-coach and Tavern Days*. Once you get used to Earle's old-fashioned curlicue prose, you realize how terrific a resource the book is—a meticulously researched and anecdotally rich chronicle of early American taverns and tavern-keepers, and of travel in the pre-railroad days. *Stage-coach and Tavern Days* is also a love letter to a bygone era that Earle and her fellow descendants of old Puritan stock saw slip away in the hubbub of the Industrial Age. Many of the taverns she mentions were still standing as the twentieth century dawned, and she knowingly describes them as you would a dear, old relative whose passing is imminent.

The successful author of many other histories, Earle "started writing ... partly because of nostalgia for more pastoral times and a patriotic urge to convey 18th-century American heroism to newly arrived immigrants," according to a *New York Times* article about Earle. She was not alone. Samuel Adams Drake's *Old Boston Taverns and Tavern Clubs*, written in 1917 with Prohibition looming, also pines for the old Yankee public house. Drake writes that the tavern is "now associated with the slums of the city and ... all may agree that as a prominent feature of society and manners, the tavern has had its day. The situation is easily accounted for. The simple truth is that in moving on the world has left the venerable institution standing in the eighteenth century."

New England demographics had changed a lot by the time Earle and Drake came of age, and so had people's drinking habits. Those "newly arrived immigrants" had never heard of flip, and they didn't have cider apple orchards growing around their tenement buildings in Boston or Lowell. They drank beer and whiskey, and they drank it in saloons. Beer still came in a wooden barrel, but instead of being made on site, as in the old tavern days, it was wheeled across town from a large factory with tall smokestacks. Beer had gone industrial.

Ice & Steam

In 1903, the editors of the Chicago-based trade journal *The Western Brewer* published a flattering profile of the Bunker Hill Breweries in Charlestown, Massachusetts, that read in part:

> In 1821 a little brick building was erected by John Cooper and Thomas Gould on Alford Street, Charlestown, near the present headquarters of the Bunker Hill breweries... This was the nucleus of the present noted plant, which covers an entire block... [The bottling department] is thoroughly equipped and up to date, and the degree of excellence attained in bottling 'P. B.' Ale, Old Musty Ale, Old Stout, Porter, Half-and-Half and Bunker Hill Lager, has had much to do in gaining the high repute they now enjoy.

The profile was part of what *The Western Brewer* called a "supplement" that chronicled the major advances in the brewing industry over the previous century. The publication is, in fact, an encyclopedic, 718-page tome titled *One Hundred Years of Brewing: A complete History of the Progress made in the Art, Science and Industry of Brewing in the World, particularly during the Nineteenth Century*. In its profiles of breweries, it offers a detailed account of America's Industrial Era beer industry—including tons of illustrations of massive brick factories and the mustachioed moguls who ran them.

The book praises Bunker Hill Breweries owner Alonzo "A. G." Van Nostrand, noting that he battled unscrupulous saloon-keepers who were selling substandard brew under the P. B. ("purest and best") label. He took eleven of those fraudsters to the Massachusetts Supreme Court, which gave these "brewers" orders to cease and desist. After describing the legal victory, *The Western Brewer* gushes, "Mr. Van Nostrand is a modern business man and has a model establishment, a combination that will always command success."

How did we get from the marginal colonial brewers whom Samuel Adams begged for decent beer so that New Englanders would stop drinking British imports, to a Boston beer baron whose product was so respected that people counterfeited it?

Somewhere around 1850, brewing in the United States began its journey into the modern age. As with other manufactured goods, the Industrial Revolution shifted production of beer from mostly small-scale producers working out of homes or modest shops, to mammoth factories in rapidly industrializing urban centers. The beverage was in demand again after decades of heavy competition from spirits and cider. To meet that demand, breweries became bigger and took advantage of a series of innovations that would mechanize production, increase output, improve distribution, boost quality, and transform brewing from an "art and mystery" to a science and a big business.

Several developments modernized brewing. The thermometer enabled people to pinpoint the ideal temperatures for drying and roasting malt and for converting malt starches to fermentable sugars during mashing. The hydrometer measured the specific gravity, or the amount of sugar, in wort—the extract from the mash that yeast ferments into beer. Brewers could thus determine not only the efficiency of their malt but also the alcoholic content of the finished beer. Later on, Louis Pasteur discovered that spoilage of fermented liquids was caused by bacteria and that those bacteria could be killed by heating, or pasteurizing, the final product. Then Emil Hansen figured out how to cultivate pure yeast strains. After thousands of years of brewing, people finally had the ability to control fermentation.

Two of the most important innovations were the steam engine and refrigeration. The steam engine mechanized brewing—and just about every other industrial process. Meanwhile, refrigeration, which originated from the New England ice trade, allowed breweries to make beer all year round.

What? There was no beer in the summer before the Industrial Revolution? There was, but it was beer that had been brewed in the colder months and stored—if you were lucky—in a cool, dark place. People had always avoided brewing during the summer. If temperatures are too warm, fermentation goes haywire. The result is off-flavors, such as that of fusel alcohols, which generally are as unpleasant as they sound.

Enter the icehouse. In 1806, a Boston entrepreneur named Frederick Tudor had the idea to harvest large chunks of ice from Fresh Pond in Cambridge, Massachusetts, and ship them to warm places like New Orleans—for profit. He was called insane. It took years of trial and error, but Tudor's idea caught on and became a viable commercial enterprise. With the invention of an ice cutter in 1825, an industry sprang up around the winter bounty of New England's ponds and lakes. You could get enough huge blocks of ice to chill an entire room or building all summer long, and that's what brewers began to do.

"The ice, thus stored, was always available for year-round fermentation," writes Stanley Baron in *Brewed in America*, adding, "The ice-room or icehouse…is spoken of as an independent development of the American brewing industry."

The words "room" or "house" don't really do justice to the architecture constructed around ice. The fermentation house of the Vienna Brewery in Roxbury, for example, was a three-story brick structure with ridiculously thick walls. Built in 1876, it was "engineered to support the weight of massed blocks of ice and rows of vats and casks," according to a Boston Landmarks Commission report. "It was common practice to site the ice chambers on the third floor, whereby blocks of ice were loaded into honeycombed compartments allowing air to circulate through. This chilled air would then settle to the bottom of the building through ventilation grates, thus cooling the fermenting tuns on the second floor and the casks on the first." Ice-based refrigeration was the standard until mechanical refrigeration made it obsolete around the turn of the nineteenth century.

The cooling of the American brewing industry is usually linked to the rise of lager brewers in the second half of the 1800s because

Ice Harvesting in Massachusetts, 1850s,
Gleason's Drawing Room Companion.

lager is generally fermented and aged at lower temperatures than ale. But most ales ferment at around 68° F—not exactly tropical—and condition best at cool temperatures. The large eastern ale brewers were actually the first to use icehouses in order to meet year-round demand for their products.

———◇———

In the early decades of the 1800s, brewing in New England was still about as primitive and small-scale as it had been since the Pilgrims landed. New York and Pennsylvania were the main beer-producing states of the era and would continue to be until the Midwest hit its stride. But the rumblings of a modern beer industry were starting in Boston and Providence.

Massachusetts and Rhode Island were the most densely settled states in the union, and their populations were growing quickly and spilling into the rest of New England (and beyond). They were also beginning a transformation from agricultural/mercantile economies to manufacturing/mercantile economies. Soon, thousands of Irish, French-Canadian, and other immigrants would join the restless farm boys and girls of the region to work in textile mills, metal shops, and shoe factories or to build turnpikes, canals, and railroads. These were the working stiffs at the vanguard of America's Industrial Revolution, and they had a powerful thirst. Their patrician bosses didn't want them getting drunk on hard liquor and slowing down production, so it was beer to the rescue.

Three notable Industrial Era breweries in New England originated in what were still the dark ages of the craft, the 1820s: the Bunker Hill Breweries and the Boston Beer Company in Boston and the Hanley Brewing Company in Providence. Another that began early in the Industrial Era, the Frank Jones Brewing Company in Portsmouth, New Hampshire, became one of the biggest, best-known breweries in the entire country.

Beyond the fact that they built a brewery on Alford Street in Charlestown (which had yet to be annexed by Boston) in 1821, little if anything is known about John Cooper and Thomas Gould. It seems they sold their enterprise to John Kent and Elias Phinney in "the days before railroads" (which arrived in the mid-1830s), according to a Charlestown historian. What Kent and Phinney had named the Mystic Lake Brewery remained "but a small affair" until William T. Van Nostrand, a malt-and-hops dealer from Brooklyn, came aboard in 1860. He eventually became the sole owner.

It was the next Van Nostrand generation that made the brewery an institution. William's son Alonzo became a full partner in 1878, when he was twenty-four. He trademarked P.B. Ale, built a separate lager brewery, and renamed the complex after the famous Revolutionary battlefield nearby. He also invested in top-of-the-line equipment. You know that bottling operation *The Western Brewer* raved about? It was part of Van Nostrand's mission to compete with Britain's world-famous Bass Ale. And apparently he did, at least in the Northeast. In 1900, he sold 892,000 bottles of ale in addition to whatever draught beer he was putting out. (Those bottles were not today's twelve-ouncers, but larger, champagne-style vessels.) One of Van Nostrand's bragging points was that P.B. Ale was the only malt liquor used at Massachusetts General and Boston City hospitals for the "sick and convalescent." Advertisements for P.B. featured a cartoon patriot and the slogan "Oh be jolly!"

Boston Brahmins embraced Van Nostrand for both his business acumen and double-barreled pedigree—his ancestors were among the first settlers of New York *and* New England. He is the only brewer included among the prominent businessmen featured in *Massachusetts of Today: A Memorial of the State, Historical and Biographical*, a book to promote the Commonwealth at the 1893 World's Fair in Chicago. Sporting an impressively bushy mustache, Van Nostrand enjoyed membership in all the right cultural societies and yacht clubs.

He died in 1923, a few years after Prohibition closed his business.

The brewery made a go at reopening when Repeal came in 1933, but it never got off the ground. P.B. Ale, Bunker Hill Lager, Boston Club Lager, Old Stout Porter, and, alas, Old Musty Ale were lost to the ages.

———◆———

The Boston Beer Company gets frequent mentions in histories on brewing because it was the oldest operating brewery in America until it closed in 1957. (That title is now held by Yuengling of Pottsville, Pennsylvania, which opened in 1829.) *The Western Brewer* explains the genesis of the brewery in 1828 as "one result of the agitation which for many years had been progressing at the Hub, in favor of the substitution of malt liquors for distilled spirits as a popular drink."

Naturally, it was a gang of Puritan descendants who took it upon themselves to produce beer in order to divert the citizenry

Courtesy of Historic New England.

from booze. Gamaliel Bradford, Nathan Rice, Benjamin Thaxter, and Elijah Loring orbited Boston's elite social and business circles. Bradford, a descendant of the *Mayflower* Bradfords, was a physician and the superintendant of Massachusetts General Hospital. He and Rice were brothers-in-law. Rice and Thaxter were partners in a prominent mercantile firm on Long Wharf. And Loring was a wealthy banker who helped launch the American School for the Deaf in Hartford.

A trove of Boston Beer Company papers that ended up in a University of Michigan library shows that the brewery was quite busy distributing ale and porter during the 1820s and 1830s. Numerous letters to Bradford from malt dealers in New York detail the price and quality of the latest barley crop. Other letters are from customers reporting whether their shipment of ale "proved good" or was "so sour it is fit for nothing except vinegar."

In addition to servicing taverns and hotels around Boston, the brewery shipped beer all over New England and as far away as New Orleans. An 1830 letter from one Crescent City client, Samuel Kathrens, offers a glimpse of contemporary attitudes toward Yankee brewing. He tells Bradford that "there is a great deal of pale ale used in this place which is brought from Philadelphia and New York and bottled here ... The people here thought there [was] no Beer made in Boston fit to drink – but after using great exertions I persuaded [the proprietor of a large hotel] to take one on trial which he found to be so far superior to what he had used that he desired me to ... keep him supplied as far as possible until you can send me some more." Kathrens puts in a request for enough barrels to supply four New Orleans hotels and "other small Bar rooms."

For some reason, in 1851, "the business of the original corporation was practically suspended," according to *The Western Brewer*. Henry F. Cox, James L. Phipps, and Henry Souther ran the place in succession until 1865, when Boston Beer was "reorganized" under a group of Irish liquor dealers looking to supply their own retail establishments. Among them was James Collins, about whom the *Boston*

Herald wrote, "Through his push and aggressiveness, ably assisted by a competent board, he increased the sales of the brewery until in 1883 the output was 117,000 barrels." At that point, Boston Beer was one of the sixteen largest breweries in the United States. Another executive who made a name for himself was Lawrence J. Logan, who became president of the brewery, was active in Democratic politics, and even fought in the Spanish-American War at the grizzled age of fifty-six. Oh, and he's the father of General Edward L. Logan, namesake of Boston's airport.

Like most breweries, Boston Beer shut down during Prohibition. And like most breweries that opened up again afterward, it limped along for awhile, probably cashing in on its "oldest brewery" fame. It made some equipment updates and started producing lager to align with younger drinkers' tastes, but St. Louis and Milwaukee had nationalized the market at that point. A relatively small, regional outfit like Boston Beer didn't stand a chance, and it closed for good in 1957. Jim Koch, brewer of Samuel Adams, resurrected the name for his company in 1984, but otherwise the old Boston Beer Company and the new one are unrelated. The sturdy brick complex on D Street in South Boston, embedded with large granite letters spelling the brewery's name, stood until 1996, when it was demolished to make way for a housing complex.

———◦———

In 1820, Otis and Oliver Holmes, two brothers from Sharon, Massachusetts, moved to Providence and built a house and a brewery on the corner of Fountain and Jackson Streets in what is today the downtown area. Like Boston, Providence in 1820 was starting to expand economically beyond shipping (and rum distilling) to manufacturing—textiles, machinery, steam engines, silverware, and jewelry. In other words, it was a good place to start a brewery. The business thrived, and after Oliver died relatively young, Otis kept things going.

He became known for activism in addition to ale. In 1842, he associated with members of Dorr's Rebellion, which sought to abolish Rhode Island's archaic property qualifications for voting. That association resulted in Otis spending fifty-nine days in prison.

Otis and two of his sons ran the brewery until 1865, at which point a saloonkeeper and wine-and-liquor dealer named John Bligh took the reigns. He built a new brewery at the Fountain-Jackson intersection and called it the Narragansett Brewery—thirty years or so before another, more famous, brewery with that name opened in Cranston. Bligh produced pale and amber beer, porter, and "hop beer" until 1875. Shortly thereafter, James Hanley stepped in and made New England beer history.

Hanley was born in Ireland in 1842 and arrived in Providence when he was four. Like Bligh, he found his initial success as a liquor dealer. With a partner and then alone, he updated and greatly expanded the brewery, eventually naming it the James Hanley Brewing Company. I'm guessing he had some editorial control over a company profile that appeared in a book on the "industries and wealth" of Rhode Island: "This company are extensive brewers of ale and porter, which are noted throughout New England for their purity and excellence. Their India Pale Ale is equal, if not superior, to any Bass or Allsop pale ale ever imported, while their Canada Malt Ale

is very rich in nutriment, a delicious family beverage, and especially adapted for invalids. Their Stock Ales and Porter cannot be excelled by any brewery in the country."

The brewery's advertising icon was the Connoisseur, a portly, middle-aged dandy making bedroom eyes at a goblet of Hanley's Peerless Ale. Pre-dating the Bud-

Courtesy of David Waugh.   weiser Clydesdales by decades,

Hanley's had a team of huge Belgian draft horses that often made appearances at fairs and parades throughout New England. After James Hanley died in 1912, his sons took over and adopted a second advertising icon, a British bulldog, a.k.a. the Watchdog of Quality. The whole quality assurance issue was not just an empty concept in those days. Until consumer-protection laws got tough, people adulterated liquor and beer to make it look aged or otherwise appealing, or they slapped someone else's label on an inferior product (as those naughty saloonkeepers did with P.B. Ale).

The Watchdog returned when Hanley's reopened after Prohibition. It was apparently sleeping on the job, however, because there were complaints of a "bitter taste, an offensive odor and a laxative effect" from those peerless ales. The company recovered and sold beer for a couple more decades until the Narragansett Brewing Company bought the brand, but not the bricks and mortar, in 1957. The brewery that started out as a humble annex of the Holmes brothers' residence in the 1820s and evolved into a modern manufacturing plant succumbed to the obsolescence of the small regional brand and to the construction of I-95. Little do the residents of today's Regency Plaza Apartments near the Dunkin' Donuts Center know that they're sleeping on the site of one of Rhode Island's longest-lived breweries.

——◇——

In 1856, an ambitious Barrington, New Hampshire farm boy, who had ventured to the bustling seaport town of Portsmouth to work for his brother's hardware store, chose a new career path that would make him a legend. He bought a sizable stake in the brewery of an Englishman, John Swindells, whose excellent ale was a hit with Portsmouth beer drinkers. Problem was, Swindells wasn't much of a businessman, so his twenty-one-year-old partner bought him out and turned the newly dubbed Frank Jones Ale into a brand name.

Jones then became a brand name himself, using his brewing success as a launchpad to a dual career as a business tycoon and a Democratic politician. He was president of the Boston & Maine Railroad (among several other corporations), a hotelier who operated the stately Rockingham and Wentworth-by-the-Sea hotels in Portsmouth and Revere House in Boston, and a real-estate baron with properties from Maine to Florida. He served two terms each as Portsmouth mayor and a New Hampshire congressman, and he missed becoming the Granite State's governor by only a few thousand votes. President Grover Cleveland considered him a friend. And those are just the highlights.

Through all that, Jones remained hands-on at the brewery—he wanted his name to be synonymous with quality ale. He built a series of successively larger and better malthouses so that the brewery could malt its own barley, for which he often traveled to Canada to buy in bulk. He also bought as much as a year's supply of hops at a time from New York and the Pacific Northwest. A spur of railroad track connected the brewery to the Boston & Maine rail line, moving supplies in and beer out of the complex on Islington Street. An average of ten freight cars full of barrels left the place each day for points throughout the East Coast (including the dry state of Maine).

A second Jones brewery operated in South Boston, and the two plants were producing over three hundred thousand barrels of ale and porter annually by the late 1880s. In those years, Frank Jones was the largest ale producer and the seventh-largest brewery in America. Its namesake was a brawny man who sported the thick facial fur that all captains of industry seemed to require. Without his gentleman's garb, he would have looked at home skinning a bear in a backwoods cabin.

Amazingly, Frank Jones was only one of three breweries in Portsmouth in the Gilded Age. Only a stone's throw from the Jones plant was the Eldredge Brewing Company, run by Jones' good friend Marcellus Eldredge. And on Bow Street, overlooking the harbor, was the Portsmouth Brewing Company, which made both ale and a lager called Portsburger. The latter two businesses were considerably smaller than the Jones brewery, but their existence says something about the thirst of a city of only eleven thousand at the time. Parts of all three breweries still stand; Portsmouth Brewing's keg-storage building is now a boutique hotel called the Ale House Inn.

Frank Jones Portsmouth Ales, courtesy of the Boston Public Library.

Frank wasn't the only Jones brewing in the Granite State, either. His younger brother opened the True W. Jones Brewery in the mill city of Manchester in 1891. Although he died in 1899, the brewery lasted until 1917.

When Frank Jones died in 1902, businesses and schools in Portsmouth closed, and two thousand mourners stood outside the church where his funeral was held. His brewery didn't reopen after Prohibition, but Frank Jones Ale lived on until 1950—ironically brewed by the Eldredge Brewing Company and then the Caldwell Distillery in Newburyport, Massachusetts. In 1989, Donald Jones, who claimed to be a descendant of the ale magnate, launched Frank Jones Portsmouth Ale through the Catamount Brewing Company of White River Junction, Vermont. It was an amber ale said to be based on one of Frank Jones' pre-Prohibition recipes. Alas, a little more than a year after Donald and his partners built their own brewing facility in Portsmouth in 1992, their business went bankrupt. The Smuttynose Brewing Company, named for one of the Isles of Shoals off the coast of Portsmouth, purchased the space.

———◆———

Breweries in the Industrial Age produced a remarkable variety of beers—pale ale, India pale ale, stock ale, amber ale, porter, lager, and bock, to name only the broad categories. There were also sub-styles like Burton and Tadcaster ales and Bohemian and Vienna lagers. The variety was especially great in New England, the only region of the country, aside from upstate New York, where ale was more popular than lager. While there are many more styles and sub-styles available among today's craft brews, that market comprises only about 7 percent of beer consumed in the United States. What beer geeks refer to as "BMC" (Bud-Miller-Coors) drinkers still represent the general taste. Things were far different in 1880, when the vast majority of beer was local and when the average New England saloon-goer was as apt to ask for a dark, hearty porter as a clear, effervescent lager.

Those two styles, porter and lager, were huge innovations in brewing. Before porter, there was just ale and beer—the latter distinguished only by a more liberal dose of hops. Porter represented a whole new category. No one really knows how it originated, but most historians do agree on when and where: 1720s London. That's when a beer made with brown malt and barrel-aged for several weeks started becoming popular. It was the color of milk chocolate and had an alcohol content of 6 to 7 percent. Working classes were said to favor this new beer, particularly the numerous "porters" who carried goods between ships, warehouses, and markets. It was the ideal liquid lunch for a laborer on the go.

Courtesy of David Waugh.

Porter was as much a sensation in the New World as it was in the Old. John Hancock, George Washington, and other gentlemen who could afford to drink imported stuff were big fans. Pennsylvania breweries were the first in America to make porters that could compete with the London brands. But the style was eclipsed in the Quaker State once German immigrants started brewing lager on a large scale. New England, on the other hand, with its largely Irish immigrant population joining the settled descendants of Englishmen, brewed porter all the way up to, and even after, Prohibition. The style lived on in Ireland as stout, which is basically a fraternal twin of porter. In the 1980s, craft brewers, inspired by imports like Guinness Export or Fuller's London Porter, resurrected the style in the United States. Just about every craft brewery in New England produces or has produced a porter or a stout.

If porter was popular, lager was revolutionary. Its coup, which in America began in the 1840s, was so complete that today beer *is* lager (or its lighter sibling pilsner) for most people around the world. Just about every global brand you can think of off the top of your head is a lager: Bud, Corona, Heineken, Beck's, Stella, Carlsburg, Tsing Dao.

Lager brewing came from Germany and produced a malt liquor very different from English ale. The late Greg Noonan, a pioneer of New England craft brewing, explains the difference in his influential 1986 book *Brewing Lager Beer*: "Lagers are defined by the process used to brew them. They are essentially distinguished from ales, the other beer family, by relatively slower fermentation at cool (40 to 55 degrees F) temperatures, followed by a relatively longer period of cold conditioning. By definition, lagers have low levels of esters [fruity flavors] and vicinal diketones [buttery notes]; devoid of significant 'yeast character,' they rely solely upon the interplay of the malt, hops, and water for their aromas and flavors."

Today's enlightened drinker often complains of lagers being insipid and one-dimensional and seeks out the more adventurous flavors of ales. Back in the mid-1800s, it was the opposite. The early adopters of lager were happy to trade ale's esters and vicinal diketones—flavors that can quickly go from adventurous to girls-gone-wild—for the cleaner character and clarity of the beer that the German newcomers were making. Developments like reliable refrigeration and the mass-production of glassware helped the lager trend, as did the locomotive. Trains were a fast new way to transport this more perishable style of beer, and refrigerated railroad cars followed soon after.

American lager brewing started in Pennsylvania and spread quickly. New England's German immigrant community was comparatively minuscule, but it created a market for lager that soon competed with the ale and porter brewers. At first, lager brewers were centered in Boston, particularly in an area with cheap land and superlative water from the Stonybrook aquifer: Roxbury and Jamaica Plain. Between the mid-1800s and Prohibition, an astonishing number of breweries—twenty-four!—operated in this area. At the dawn of the twentieth century, Boston had a total of thirty-one breweries—the most per capita in the nation. These weren't the primitive, tavern-oriented facilities of yore. They were multi-story, thick-walled factories turning out tens or hundreds of thousands of barrels per year for a rapidly growing populace that was guzzling beer like mad.

Roessle, Burkhardt, Pfaff, Haffenreffer. These are the guys whose lagers competed with Boston ales. John Roessle was the first lager brewer in Boston in 1846. Gottlieb F. Burkhardt came along in 1850 and shrewdly gave his brews labels like Red Sox Beer and Pennant Ale. Bavarian brothers Henry and Jacob Pfaff proudly proclaimed their lager a "Boston production." And Rudolph Haffenreffer, who started out working for Burkhardt, built a New England beer empire that lasted until 1964. There were a few savvy non-Germans who decided it made good business sense to brew lager: A.J. Houghton, a Readsboro, Vermont native who owned the Vienna Brewery (with its aforementioned ice-cooled fermentation room), and John Kenney, an Irish immigrant who started the Union Brewery and American Brewing Company along with the ale-producing Park Brewery.

Boston Beer Company in South Boston, 1880,
courtesy of the Boston Public Library.

Henry Rueter was the rare German who brewed ale. He teamed up with an Irishman named John Alley to form the Highland Spring Brewery, which was the largest ale and porter brewery in America in the 1870s and one of the first breweries to adopt artificial refrigeration. Rueter was also president of the United States Brewers Association from 1876 to 1881. Launched in 1862 when the newly established Internal Revenue Service imposed new taxes on beer to finance the Civil War, the association became a prominent lobbying group for the brewing industry. Rueter strengthened the organization's stance against temperance reformers. One of the first things he did as president was get a Brewers Hall included in the Centennial Exhibition in Philadelphia—the first World's Fair held in the United States—triumphing over attempts to ban beer at the event. One wonders if he tried to act surprised when Highland Spring Ale won first prize in the exhibition's beer competition.

In large part because of the popularity of lager, the number of breweries in the United States jumped from 431 to 1,269 between 1850 and 1860. Then things really took off. By 1870, there were 3,286 breweries, although consolidation and temperance politics brought that number down to 1,345 by 1915. Total beer production increased from 3.6 million barrels in 1865 to over 66 million barrels in 1914. Accordingly, per capita consumption skyrocketed during that period from 3.2 gallons to 18.7 gallons. (Lest you think we're living in a less beery era, per capita consumption in 2012 was 28.3 gallons.)

New England had an estimated eighty breweries at the beginning of the twentieth century, a number that likely omits many that were producing on a smaller scale. Some brewed ale, some brewed lager, and many brewed both, along with the numerous sub-styles within those two beer families. Here's a sort of highlight reel of an era when every New England city seemed to have at least one brewery:

The Hull Brewing Company was the longest-running brewery in Connecticut, lasting from 1872 to 1977. It was one of twelve breweries in New Haven before Prohibition, which placed the Elm City second to Boston as a New England beer mecca. Post-Prohibition, Hull moved into a complex that once housed the Philip Fresenius Sons' brewery. The latter started out in 1852 as the first Industrial Age brewery in New Haven (and one of the first in Connecticut). Established by the German lager brewer Philip Fresenius and then stewarded by his sons Henry and Philip, it was the largest beer producer in the city before Prohibition. When Philip Jr. died in 1910, he made headlines by leaving a will that gave only $5 to each of his surviving relatives and the rest of his estate, worth $350,000, to his wife, Charlotte. The Fresenius family had snubbed the couple, presumably because Charlotte, "a beauteous woman of New Orleans ... was, prior to her marriage, engaged in a most sporty occupation," the *Bridgeport Herald* snickered.

Another New Haven beer institution was the Quinnipiac Brewery, later named the Yale Brewing Company. Situated in a picturesque spot on the Quinnipiac River, this brewery was big enough to have its own train track for moving goods in and out. It had no connection to the Ivy League university, which amazingly didn't balk at sharing a name with a brewery. Owner A.W. Kendall served as president of the United States Brewers Association from 1901 to 1903. The brewery's 1896-era buildings have been converted into a handsome waterfront apartment complex called Brewery Square.

Among Hartford's four breweries, the biggest was the New England Brewing Company (nicknamed NEBCO), to which a modern Connecticut craft brewery of the same name pays tribute. There was also the Aetna Brewing Company, Hartford's longest-lived brewery, which opened in 1865, made near beer during Prohibition, and closed in 1947. In New Britain in 1905, a Lithuanian immigrant and tavern owner named John Skritulsky established a brewery with the excellent name Cremo whose popular ales and lagers made it until 1955. Allowed to produce near beer during Prohibition, the brewery was busted for making the real thing and had to pay a $100,000 fine.

In western Massachusetts, the Springfield area along the Connecticut River was home to five beer manufacturers: the Highland, Liberty, and Springfield breweries in Springfield, and the Consumers and Hampden breweries in Chicopee. Springfield was an industrial city whose armory pioneered mass-production manufacturing. It also invented basketball. How could it not love beer? All five breweries eventually consolidated to become the Springfield Breweries Company, which produced 350,000 barrels of ale and lager annually at its peak and was very un-Yankee in proclaiming itself "New England's greatest brewing institution."

There *were* a few great things about Springfield Breweries. Among its owners was Franklin Pierce, the grandson and namesake of the New Hampshire-born fourteenth U.S. president, and Theodor Geisel, grandfather of one of New England's literary giants, Dr. Seuss (whose name was also Theodor Geisel and who would later illustrate advertisements for the Narragansett Brewing Company). Also, one of the company's branches, the Springfield Brewing Company, won a gold medal for its Tivoli Beer in Baden-Baden, Germany in 1896, besting 125 other German and American competitors. Perhaps most memorable of all is the advertising icon for the Hampden Brewery (the only one to reopen after Prohibition): the Handsome Waiter, a skinny, old, bald dude in tails. In his 1988 book *Beer New England*, Will Anderson notes that, perhaps because of "the region's dry sense of humor ... the brewers of New England—more than any other section of the country—have made use of less than Calvin Klein types" in their advertising.

The Commonwealth's second-largest city, Worcester, had two major breweries, the best-known being Bowler Brothers, which opened in 1883. John and Alexander Bowler immigrated to America from Ipswich, England, and learned the brewing trade from their father. The popularity of their Tadcaster Ale made them rich, and they built a summer estate on the ocean in Gloucester that is now a resort on the National Register of Historic Places.

New Bedford had Dawson's, which another English immigrant, Benjamin Dawson, started with his son, Joseph, in 1899. The brewery would achieve greater fame after Prohibition with its slogan "Time Out for Dawson's!" and as the first brewery to sponsor Red Sox games on the radio.

Another Massachusetts producer to flourish both before and after the dry years was the Harvard Brewing Company of Lowell. Originating as the Consumers Brewing Company in 1894, it soon became not only the biggest brewery in New England but also "one of the finest and best-equipped breweries in the United States," declared the trade journal *The Western Brewer*. Like the Yale Brewing Company in New Haven, the Harvard Brewing Company was both unconnected to and unprotested by the famous university. Harvard University reacted differently a hundred years later, however, when the Lowell

Brewing Company revived the Harvard brand for a new lager in 1998. It threatened to sue the brewery—college binge drinking was all over the news—and nervous retailers took the product off their shelves. The revival was short-lived.

—◇—

Rhode Island had five major breweries in addition to Hanley's, including, of course, Narragansett. If New Englanders are going to remember any of the region's old industrial beers, they're going to remember Narragansett, which made it all the way to 1983 and was resurrected in 2005. (More on 'Gansett in Chapter Six, *Bottles & Cans*.) I also can't help but mention the What Cheer Brewing Company in Cranston. Started in 1868 by the Molter family, the brewery's name comes from the famous Ocean State phrase that originated with the Narragansett Indians' words of welcome to Rhode Island founder Roger Williams in 1636: "What cheer, netop?".

As discussed earlier, New Hampshire had a thriving brewing industry in Portsmouth, which spilled into Manchester for a bit. Tiny North Walpole opened a five-story brewery in 1876 that started out as Walker, Blake & Company and had several subsequent names, including Fall Mountain Lager Company and Mountain Spring Brewing Company. North Walpole is right across the Connecticut River from Bellows Falls, Vermont, which housed the brewery's headquarters. Other than this dual-state operation, Industrial Era brewing didn't exist in Vermont. After all, the Green Mountain State wasn't industrial, and it hopped aboard the temperance wagon early. Hell, it helped build the temperance wagon.

The same is true of the Pine Tree State, whose 1851 Maine Law was the first prohibition law in the country. Yet, beginning in 1858, some bold entrepreneurs in Portland managed to get around the ban with two notable malt-liquor enterprises: the Forest City Brewery and the Casco Brewery. Involved in both were James

"Handsome Jim" McGlinchy and his brothers, who cut a swath through the city in not only the beer but also the saloon, liquor, retail, and landlord businesses. There were loopholes in the Maine Law as well as lapses in enforcement, and the brothers exploited them with gangster-esque panache.

There had to be a little McGlinchy in every New England brewer of the late 1800s and early 1900s. While their industry boomed and they were admired as entrepreneurs, they all frequently ran up against fits of temperance. The earliest steps toward national Prohibition were taken by New England states, where the Puritan mentality battled its own predilection toward sin. This climate created uncertainty about the future of the brewers' considerable investments.

"Legal hindrances to beer traffic have always been a feature of New England legislation, and kept brewers very largely to local needs. It prevented the growth that is so marked in this trade around St. Louis, Detroit, Philadelphia, and New York, where more liberal policies prevailed." That's how the *Boston Herald* aptly summed up the Yankee beer industry in *Commercial and Financial New England*, a special publication celebrating the region's economic prowess. And that was in 1906, when brewing was at its height!

After Prohibition, a handful of local or regional brands would keep alive the concept of a "New England beer," but before long everyone would pledge allegiance to Schlitz or Ballantine. Who remembered P.B. and Highland Spring ales or Fresenius and Tivoli lagers? More importantly, in a modern era when national brands were the Best New Thing, who cared?

Alcohol

The alcohol content of beer ranges from roughly 3 percent to 12 percent. Most mass-produced brands fall in the 4-to-5-percent range. Bud Light, the best-selling beer in America, has 4.2 percent alcohol, while "Bud Heavy," as the kids call Budweiser these days, has 5 percent. The heavily hopped, "double" IPAs that craft beer drinkers can't get enough of average about 8 percent. A Belgian tripel or an English barleywine can get up to 11 or 12 percent, but those are rare.

For the most part, beer is the weakest alcoholic beverage, which puts it in an ambiguous position when it comes to efforts to control drinking. If you think of anti-alcohol groups as parents and drinkers as teenagers, you can get a pretty good handle on the entire history of America's attitude toward beer. Parents don't want teenagers to drink at all. They know that beer can lead to hard liquor and drugs or cause reckless behavior all on its own. But when the cops crash a high-school party and find only empty bottles of PBR, parents may be kind of relieved. *Well, at least the kids weren't doing tequila shots...*

Such equivocation over beer began the moment the Puritans arrived and made New England the world capital of regulated boozing.

It's true that New England's earliest settlers could not imagine life without beer. It was their universal beverage—a substitute for water, a liquid form of bread, a delivery vehicle for herbal medicine. Some of their first laws mandated a reliable, affordable, quality beer supply. The authorities believed that if people could get decent beer at a fair price, they wouldn't be seduced by "strong waters," a.k.a. hard liquor.

The Puritans weren't fools, though. They were well aware that you could get drunk on beer, and drunkenness was not tolerated. "Drink is in itself a good creature of God and is to be received with thankfulness, but the abuse of drink is from Satan," the minister Increase Mather declared. While still living in England, future Massachusetts Bay Colony governor John Winthrop proposed a bill to the House of Commons, "For Preventing Drunkenness." He argued that the potency of beer should be controlled "to that proportion of strength, as may be wholesome for our bodye, and not influencing to drunkenness."

Hangover from hell. Puritans punished their more enthusiastic drinkers with a night in the stocks.

Within four years of the Puritans' arrival in Massachusetts, there were enough taverns, and enough people in them getting drunk on beer, that the General Court enacted a law requiring innkeepers to get their beer from a licensed brewer instead of making their own. Presumably, some of these innkeepers had been making malt liquors potent enough to be "influencing to drunkenness." The problem with the new rule was that there was only one licensed brewer in the entire Bay Colony, Captain Robert Sedgwick of Charlestown, and his output couldn't keep up with demand. Cue the unintended consequences.

"By restricting the manufacture of beer," writes Stanley Baron in *Brewed in America*, the Puritans "probably brought about a shortage which, in turn, led to an increase in the use of spirits—the very opposite of their intention." The new law was revoked, and innkeepers went back to brewing as they pleased.

The duel between our Yankee ancestors' fondness for drink and their anxiety over its ill effects became the basis of a peculiarly American mentality toward alcohol that culminated in Prohibition.

——◆——

During the decades of temperance agitation that led to the Great Experiment, the argument over beer was basically *It's the drink of moderation! No! Wait! It's a milder strain of demon rum!* The latter view was first given serious consideration in Boston in 1826 by the newly formed American Society for the Promotion of Temperance. This was a religious movement spearheaded by Justin Edwards, pastor of the Park Street Church, and other prominent men of the cloth, including the presidents of Yale and Brown Universities. In a departure from earlier temperance reformers, who merely preached against the use of ardent spirits, this lot decided that "the only logical basis of the temperance movement is entire abstinence from *all* intoxicants." At that point the original meaning of temperance, i.e. moderation, went out the window.

"At the outset [the movement] obtained its greatest support in New England, where a peculiarly Puritan (in the modern, not the original, sense) strain of social responsibility, abstemiousness, sanctimony, do-goodism and moral severity—all uncomfortably and incompatibly combined—had taken hold. It was also part of the general reform fervor of the nineteenth century, and in case after case its adherents supported abolition and women's rights as well," writes Baron. OK, two out of three worthy causes ain't bad. And let's face it, while the goal of abstinence was doomed to failure, the thinking behind it was cutting-edge for its time and widely accepted today: Whether they drink whiskey or beer, alcoholics are alcoholics, and their only path to sobriety is to lay off the sauce entirely.

One of the first attempts to legislate sobriety was Massachusetts' Fifteen Gallon Law of 1838, which banned hard liquor sales of less than that amount. It was really a ploy to legislate the sobriety of the working classes who bought booze by the shot in dram shops and "tippling houses," not the upper classes who could afford to purchase liquor in bulk and tipple privately in their mansions and clubs. The law was so unpopular and obviously discriminatory that it was repealed within a couple of years.

But the anti-liquor forces were undaunted by the Fifteen Gallon Law's failure. Just as they had progressed from temperance to abstinence, they were moving beyond moral persuasion and sobriety pledges to the rule of law. The "local option" to allow municipalities to vote themselves "wet" or "dry" became popular and was especially effective in Massachusetts—by 1842, there was only one county that licensed the sale of hard liquor. Then Maine did something radical. It took the local option statewide and enacted the nation's first total ban on alcoholic beverages. Neal Dow, the "Father of Prohibition," led the way.

Dow was raised in Portland by strict Quaker parents who strove to keep him on a righteous path, even forbidding him from attending college at Bowdoin for fear of corrupting influences he might encounter there. His maternal great-grandfather's first name was, I kid you not, Hate-Evil. Through the tannery that his father started and turned over to his son, Dow got a close look at the lives of laborers. The thing that struck him most was their rampant boozing.

In his memoirs, he writes, "I saw health impaired, capacity undermined, employment lost. I saw wives and children suffering from the drinking habits of husbands and fathers ... My indignation at the men who brought so much suffering upon their families for the gratification, as it then seemed to me, of a mere taste for liquor softened into pity and sympathy

Neal Dow, daguerreotype, circa 1850.

when I found them the apparently helpless victims of a controlling appetite that was dragging them to ruin."

Like a lot of temperance crusaders, Dow appeared at first to be reacting reasonably to what was going on at the time. Boozing was rampant. In the 1800s, Americans consumed about three times as much alcohol as they do today. It was common practice, for example, for laborers to receive liquor as part of their pay. The City of Portland actually rang a bell to alert workers of their 11 a.m. and 4 p.m. rum breaks. Dow led a group of Portland employers to call for an end to this custom and allow workers to collect actual wages in place of liquid ones. *Hey, maybe these guys wouldn't drink so much if their bosses weren't pushing hooch on them all the time.* But curbing excesses like workplace drinking was just the beginning.

Dow planned to boldly go where no man had gone before. He helped several prohibitionists get elected to the Maine legislature and then strong-armed that body to pass a statewide ban on alcoholic beverages when he was elected mayor of Portland in 1851. With this development, the temperance movement officially jumped to the next level. Dow became a national celebrity and a hero to drys who hadn't dared dream of bending the political system to their will. As one historian put it, "Until then the movement had been a primarily spiritual crusade striving for the millennium of universal personal abstinence; from that point forward it became primarily a political campaign directed toward an ultimate goal of universal legal prohibition."

Soon thereafter, other states enacted similar laws. Rhode Island, Massachusetts, and Vermont jumped on the wagon in 1852, followed by Connecticut in 1854 and New Hampshire in 1855.

Then came the Portland Rum Riot. In June 1855, an angry crowd of three thousand, many of them Irish immigrants who hated Dow and his Maine Law, gathered around City Hall. Dow called in the militia to disperse the mob, and a struggle ensued in which the militia killed one man and wounded seven others. It turned out prohibition had an ugly side: enforcement.

Because of that, and because abolition trumped temperance as a political cause, most states repealed their prohibition laws. However, Vermont's dry status, though poorly enforced, lasted until a local option passed in 1902. Massachusetts see-sawed, repealing prohibition in 1868, reenacting it in 1869, and repealing it again in 1875. And the Maine Law stayed on the books in one form or another right up until the repeal of national Prohibition in 1933. That would have been a consolation to Dow, whose heavy-handed crackdown on the rum rioters cast a pall over the rest of his career.

———◇———

Even though the Civil War bumped temperance to the political back burner, prohibitionists had already influenced the culture: drinking became temperate in the sense that people switched to beer from spirits. This change was also, in much of the country, due to the popularity of lager, which German immigrants introduced in the 1840s. Ironically, the Internal Revenue Act of 1862, which taxed beer at a dollar per barrel to fund the Civil War, strengthened the beer industry. It spurred brewers to get organized and form their own lobbying group, the United States Brewers Association (USBA). Between 1850 and 1870, the number of breweries in the United States exploded from 431 to 3,286. Between 1865 and 1914, per capita consumption of beer skyrocketed from 3.2 gallons to 18.7 gallons. Sales of spirits, meanwhile, fell by half.

At no other time than today did New England have as many breweries. Boston, New Haven, Providence, Springfield, and Portsmouth (New Hampshire) were beer hubs, and many other towns with commercial or industrial activity boasted their own local brands. (The fact that dozens of breweries opened in New England while prohibition laws were still on the books says a lot about how difficult and/or lax enforcement was.)

Where was all this beer being drunk? Saloons, mostly. In industrialized areas, the inns and taverns of Olde New England were giving way to a new kind of watering hole patronized primarily by immigrants and the working class.

"The typical saloon featured offerings besides drink and companionship," writes Daniel Okrent in *Last Call: The Rise and Fall of Prohibition* (2010). "In these places, where a customer's ties to a neighborhood might be new and tenuous, saloonkeepers cashed paychecks, extended credit, supplied a mailing address or a message drop for men who had not yet found a permanent home, and in some instances provided sleeping space at five cents a night." Another historian notes, "Politics were also part of the saloon ... because there were few alternative locations for partisan discussion."

Sound familiar? Like the taverns of the colonial era, saloons were social, economic, and political institutions essential to helping immigrants from the Old World get a foothold in the New World. In Worcester, for example, the primary immigrant groups were Irish, German, French-Canadian, English, and Swedish—and each had its own saloons, as did working-class Yankees. In the 1880s, the

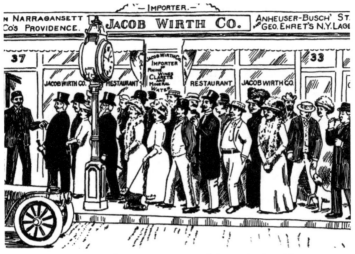

Lining up for a pint. Postcard from the booklet
A Seidel for Jake Wirth.

industrial coastal city of Bridgeport, Connecticut had nearly three hundred drinking establishments, or one for every fifteen men.

These new drinking spaces were more commercial than the taverns of yore. Breweries had evolved into big businesses, and with so many of them clustered in urban centers, competition was fierce. Meanwhile, saloonkeepers were classic small business owners, launching their enterprises on a shoestring. So brewers would often fund these startups in exchange for exclusive rights to the tap lines. And by "fund," I mean they would foot the bill for everything from the tap lines to the furniture to the painting of the buxom beauty on the wall. Often they would provide loans. The breweries needed to move product, and the saloonkeepers and their customers said, "Bring it on." (Such "pay to play" practices by breweries and wholesalers are illegal today, although suspicions that some companies skirt the law arise pretty regularly.)

Temperance crusaders did not applaud beer's comeback as an improvement over decades of hard boozing. Beer had lost its innocence now that it was associated with the drys' nemesis, the saloon. The most prominent prohibitionist group in America was called the Anti-Saloon League for a reason. Sure, a fair number of these barrooms were gritty. Noise, gambling, prostitution, and the odors of stale beer and fresh vomit were oft-cited offenses. But saloon bashing had as much to do with fear of alien hordes as concern over vice. Native New Englanders viewed the largest immigrant group, Irish Catholics, with increased anxiety as each successive wave threatened Anglo-Protestant dominance. The Irish were stereotyped as pathological drunks who plotted to take over local politics from their barstools. With that scenario in their heads, prohibitionists targeted not only saloons but also the breweries that underwrote them.

In his annual report of 1873, Boston police chief Edward Savage included an essay, "A View of Intemperance, From a Police Stand-Point," in which he expressed frustration in combating the crime of drunkenness. He described an experiment in which he instructed his officers to ask everyone arrested for the crime during one summer month, "What did you drink?" The top answers were whiskey (440), beer (316), whiskey and beer (93), everything (91), rum (45), and gin (36) in addition to such arbitrary retorts as "castor oil," "don't know," and "none of your business."

Savage used the poll to publicly condemn local brewers. He snidely remarks, "One curious feature that crops out in the revelation made by [those arrested] invites the inquiry, how is it that so many get drunk on beer?—that harmless beverage that contains so little of the intoxicating properties."

The brewers probably had a chuckle over Savage's unintentionally hilarious "exit polls" and then calmly went back to putting out propaganda like, "The tonic tang of prime hops and the purest malted grain invigorates and strengthens" and that a particular brew "is very rich in nutriment, a delicious family beverage, and especially adapted for invalids."

Brewers had been marketing their product as wholesome since the first temperance meeting. Public relations by the USBA and trade journals such as *The Western Brewer* played up beer's image as the drink of moderation (and health!) while throwing spirits under the bus. The latter caused "domestic misery, pauperism, disease and crime," while the former was "not only the purest of all beverages, but also the most beneficial to the body and mind."

And like any controversial but powerful industry, brewers flexed their political muscle when necessary. For the USBA convention of 1874, which was held in Boston, Hub lager brewer Henry Pfaff, New Hampshire ale-brewer Frank Jones (who was also, conveniently, a congressman at the time), and Philadelphia ale-brewer William Massey drafted an "Address to the People of the United States" that raised a new, compelling argument: If you shut down the brewing industry, who will finance the U.S. government? Good point. The industry contributed about 20 percent of annual federal revenue.

The New England brewers especially loved calling out the hypocrisy of their states' temperance laws, which included exemptions for hard cider and fruit wines—beverages produced and consumed by prohibitionist politicians' rural constituency. They must have cheered at the 1871 convention when the USBA's attorney in Washington, D.C., Louis Schade, caricatured the Yankees' "secret" drinking habit.

"Some of the so-called temperance States consume more beer, in spite of their temperance laws, than even the Western or German States ... Who would have believed that our Yankee friends in New Hampshire drink just as much beer as the Pennsylvanians ... And pious Massachusetts, where is she? Do her people drink, too? Puritanical Massachusetts, the seat of two-thirds of all the piety in the

*Dumping barrels of beer after a raid, courtesy of
the Library of Congress.*

country; the home of the principal temperance agitators; the hot-bed of all the great moral ideas with which the country lately has been blessed—Massachusetts, the land of the Pilgrims, not only drinks, but she drinks hard—ninety-nine glasses of beer per head during the year. True, however, to herself and her reputation, she only *drinks on the sly*!"

Mocking those two-faced drys would take the USBA only so far. The brewers were politically outmatched by the Anti-Saloon League, which Okrent refers to as the "mightiest pressure group in the nation's history." In 1909, Gallus Thomann, the manager of the USBA's "literary arm," wrote that "there can be no doubt that brewing has suffered in all parts of the country where the Anti-Saloon movement has succeeded."

The passage of the income tax to mitigate lost revenue from the alcoholic beverage industry helped the Anti-Saloon movement. What sealed the deal, however, was America's involvement in World War I and the accompanying anti-German hysteria. (Outside of New England, the brewing industry was almost entirely run by men of German heritage.) In 1919, four New England states joined the majority that voted to save Americans from themselves, ratifying the eighteenth amendment to the Constitution that prohibited "the manufacture, sale, or transportation of intoxicating liquors." Connecticut and Rhode Island, whose populations were 67 and 76 percent Catholic, respectively, were the only two states to reject the amendment.

From 1920 to 1933, all of America learned what Maine had when it enacted prohibition way back in 1851: enforcement's a bitch. "The liquor industry wasn't dead, of course; a new version, this one illegal, underground, and nearly ubiquitous, would emerge with the birth of the dry utopia," writes Okrent. Lots of whiskey and rum passed through—surprise!—Maine via the coastline and the Canadian border on its way to points throughout the Northeast.

The beer industry, on the other hand, was effectively dead. The weakest alcoholic beverage is also the least valuable and the bulkiest, so beer wasn't popular as a bootlegged item. And it's pretty hard to operate a brewery in secret. The rivers of ale and lager that kept saloons afloat were gone. Now it was gin in flasks slipping through the doors of speakeasies. Everyone was back on the hard stuff again.

Bottles & Cans

Jeff Browning, who brews beer at the New Haven, Connecticut nightclub-brewpub-pizzeria BAR, remembers when collecting beer cans was a popular hobby. As a kid in the mid-1970s, he accidentally locked himself out of his house early one morning while delivering newspapers. Prompted by a friend who'd started a beer can collection, Browning figured he'd kill time by picking up cans along the road before heading home to rouse his sleeping family. "By the time my parents woke up, I had, like, thirty-eight different beer cans," he says. It was the beginning of a serious habit.

Nowadays, Browning's house is essentially a museum of beer cans and all manner of brewery memorabilia, or "breweriana." He specializes in Connecticut breweries and has what is certainly the world's largest collection of beer artifacts from the Nutmeg State. Looking at walls and shelves chock full of vintage advertisements for

Aetna, Cremo, Hull, Red Fox, and Wehle "Mule Head" beer, you might marvel at the fact that Browning's collection represents only a handful of the thousands of forgotten American breweries. There are serious collectors like him all over the country, and their nerdy passion has made breweriana a significant niche in the antique market. One New England collector recently sold a pair of sought-after cans for $35,000.

Money doesn't drive this crowd as much as history and nostalgia. Enthusiasts share knowledge and trade objects through groups such as the Eastern Coast Breweriana Association, whose staid motto is, "Through breweriana the history of the brewing industry will be preserved." Launched in 1970, ECBA publishes a quarterly magazine, *The Keg*, and organizes numerous shows and conventions each year. The proliferation of craft breweries in recent decades has breathed new life into the hobby, and many new collectors specialize in craft beer memorabilia from their hometown or state.

Will Anderson, who started collecting beer cans as a Cornell University student in 1961, co-founded the ECBA and coined the term breweriana. A longtime resident of Connecticut and Maine, he made a name for himself in 1973 with *The Beer Book*, whose neighborly prose and color images celebrated the bygone local brews of America that had been supplanted by a handful of homogenized megabrands with national advertising campaigns. The book netted Anderson interviews on the *Today Show* and in *Town & Country*.

Anderson's quirky term for brewery memorabilia debuted in the title of his 1969 book, *Beers, Breweries & Breweriana*. "The 'Beers' stood for beer bottles, the 'Breweries' stood for all the breweries that existed across America at one time or another, and the 'Breweriana' stood for all those trays and cans and bottles and signs—and all their color and pizzazz," he wrote in the foreword to another book, *New England Breweriana* (2001). That book was compiled by a group of collectors (including Browning) whose trays and cans and bottles and signs—and tap knobs and lithographs and bottle openers and foam scrapers—are fascinating relics of New England's rich brewing culture before and just after Prohibition.

Anderson, who now lives in Bath, Maine, wrote the scrapbook-style histories *Beer New England* (1988) and *The Great State of Maine Beer Book* (1996). In addition to breweriana from around the country, his house contains treasures like a photo of him with Willie Mays and a plastic rocket salvaged from a dismantled ride at Coney Island. Anderson likes nothing better than to go on road trips, stay in old motels, and visit diners, ballparks, roadside attractions, and, yes, breweries. He loves Americana, and he borrowed from that word to invent a unique term for old beer stuff—and all its "color and pizzazz."

—◇—

Bottles came before cans. Bottled beer has been around since at least the 1700s, but it was uncommon in the United States until the late 1800s and wasn't prevalent until after Prohibition. Anheuser-

The Narragansett bottling line, courtesy of Narragansett Beer.

Busch pioneered bottling on a large scale in 1873 when it adopted Louis Pasteur's method of flash-heating bottled beer to kill bacteria. This meant that the product could be shipped long distances without spoiling. Thus began the gradual transformation of the brewing industry from local businesses making fresh draft beer for surrounding communities to an industry dominated by a few mass-produced brands engineered to survive journeys along the global supply chain.

Even if they didn't distribute beyond their local markets, American breweries that bottled beer followed Anheuser-Busch's lead and adopted pasteurization. As demand for beer in general surged in the late 1800s, so did demand for bottled beer. The invention of the "crown" cap in 1892 allowed bottles to be sealed by machine rather than corked by hand. Many breweries didn't do their own bottling at first—they outsourced it to glass manufacturers that specialized in the activity. In Boston, some of those companies organized as the Bottlers' and Soda Manufacturers' Association and were so allied with brewers that they lobbied against statewide prohibition in Massachusetts in 1873.

Speaking of soda manufacturers, it was they who enabled breweries to bottle on a much larger scale after Prohibition. They had advanced the technology during the dry years to meet the demands of consumers who brought bottles of pop home to chill in the icebox. Similarly, in the 1930s and 1940s, beer was increasingly purchased for home consumption at large, new stores called supermarkets. By 1941, packaged beer outsold draft, which today accounts for less than 10 percent of sales.

Hanley's cone top, courtesy of David Waugh.

Beer's domestication was also made possible by the beer can, which came along in 1935. Starting with the American Can Company, several can makers pounced on the beer market in the mid-1930s. The tin containers were "keglined"—coated with a Union Carbide product called Vinylite—which supposedly prevented the beer inside from tasting like metal. (Devotees of bottles dismissed that notion for decades.) Brewers who adopted cans early on trumpeted the advantages of the new container. It was only used once and required no deposit (unlike bottles in those days), which also meant that no one else's mouth had ever touched the can—a selling point for the germ-conscious. It blocked

Women were able to carry a six-pack all by themselves, courtesy private collection.

light, which turns beer skunky by causing a chemical reaction in compounds found in hops. Plus, it was lightweight and stackable, and you didn't need a separate label. For a little while, "cone top" cans filled a niche for smaller brewers who couldn't afford canning machinery; they had a conical spout and a crown seal so that they could be filled with existing bottling equipment. Breweriana collectors go nutty for cone tops, as they were only around for ten years or so.

Finally, with cans came the six-pack. Why the six-pack? Manufacturers decided that was the maximum number of 12-ounce containers that a woman could comfortably carry out of the supermarket. (You might say the six-pack has been the beer industry's only significant attempt to consider the female consumer.) The new packaging also presented a convenient way to advertise the product within. "In the days of draught beer, the customer never saw or examined the barrel, so there was no need to make it distinctive or dress it up," writes Stanley Baron in *Brewed in America*. "But the bottle and the can were quite different: they were handled by the customer and had to attract by their covers, so to speak, and so all the resources of labeling, coloring and design had to be called into play."

With the help of attractive packaging and other marketing, breweries made a robust comeback after Repeal despite the dire economics of the Great Depression. By 1934, there were 756 companies making beer across the country. But the post-Prohibition beer business would soon be defined by size instead of geography. The big companies grew bigger through mergers and acquisitions, and the number of breweries started to shrink. By 1940, there were only 684. World War II and its shortages of raw materials, such as barley, further strained many breweries. Companies adapted to the shortage by using a greater percentage of adjunct grains—corn and rice, primarily—to barley malt, which resulted in beer that was not only lighter in body but also less expensive to produce. Brewers stuck with adjuncts after the war and increased their profit margins. Consumers didn't mind the lighter beers—they seemed to demand them, in

Theodore Haffenfreffer (standing) admires a display of bottles of Pickwick Ale brewed in Boston, courtesy of the Haffenreffer family.

fact. Post-war brews were consistently, perhaps comfortingly, bland.

The consolidation of the beer business further accelerated so that by the late 1970s, there remained in the United States only forty-four brewing companies—the top four of which would claim 94 percent of the market by 2001. Beer had officially become a mass-produced commodity whose hometown mattered way less than its exposure in magazines and billboards and on radio and TV.

———◆———

The 1940s through the 1960s was the last hurrah of New England breweries with Industrial Era roots—the ones whose brands you might have glimpsed on an old can or baseball program in your grandparents' basement: Narragansett, Hull, and Pickwick. Dawson's, Hampden, and Holihan. The most successful New England brewers of this era, or of any era since, were the Haffenreffers.

Pretty much the only reason contemporary beer drinkers recognize that name is because of Haffenreffer Private Stock Malt Liquor, a.k.a. P-Stock, Haffenwrecker, and Green Death. The 2010 *Boston Globe* obituary headline for the Harvard-trained biochemist who formulated Private Stock was, I'm not kidding, "August Haffenreffer, 94; concocted potent 'Green Death' beer." Ironically, Private Stock was marketed as a super-premium lager for the country club set when it debuted in the 1950s. It was "the malt liquor with the imported taste," and ads featured a debonair waiter holding a tray with a couple of green 40-ounce bottles and some pilsner glasses.

But at some point, P-Stock left the country club and acquired a reputation as a cheap way to get a good buzz. In the 1970s, Wilt Chamberlain appeared in ads endorsing the beer's potency ("Nobody does it bigger"), and in the 1990s, Tupac Shakur and the Notorious B.I.G. enshrined Private Stock in rap songs. With an alcohol content that was traditionally about 7 percent—greater than most mass-market lagers but tame compared to many of today's craft brews—Haffenwrecker gets a 74, or "okay," rating on BeerAdvocate.com. Whatever you think of Private Stock, it is, along with Narragansett Lager, the last remnant of the Haffenreffers' once expansive repertoire.

During its hundred years in the brewing business, the family owned not only Haffenreffer & Co. in Boston's Jamaica Plain neighborhood but Old Colony/Enterprise Brewing in Fall River, Massachusetts and the Narragansett Brewing Co. in Cranston, Rhode Island—the most successful New England-based brewery ever. They also bought the venerable Hanley Brewing Co. of Providence and the Croft Ale Brewery of Roxbury, Massachusetts, shutting down both but continuing to produce the companies' brands in Cranston. Haffenreffer-produced beers included Boh (short for Bohemian, a Czech-style pilsner), Boylston, Croft, Hanley, Haffenreffer, Krueger (a New Jersey brand that was the first canned beer), Pickwick, and Narragansett—in a variety of styles. These included lager and its lighter sibling pilsner, bock (a strong, honey-ish lager traditionally released in spring), pale ale, cream ale, export ale, porter, and stout. With their beer-based fortune, the Haffenreffers purchased the Herreshoff yacht company, which produced eight America's Cup vessels, and were benefactors of Brown University in Providence.

The man who started it all was Rudolph Haffenreffer, who immigrated to America from Württemburg, Germany in 1868. Already an experienced brewer at age twenty-one, he began working at Gottlieb F. Burkhardt's in Roxbury, one of Boston's first lager breweries. Pure water from the Stonybrook aquifer, along with cheap land, made Roxbury and Jamaica Plain a magnet for brewers, and that area became a hub of New England's small German immigrant population. Rudolph quickly worked his way up to brewmaster and married Catherine Burkhardt, Gottlieb's seventeen-year-old niece.

In 1870, he started the Boylston Brewery on Bismarck and Germania streets in Jamaica Plain, though it was soon thereafter known as Haffenreffer & Co. At first, he brewed only lagers, but in 1901—this being New England, after all—ales and porters joined the portfolio. At that point, the plant had expanded from a modest wooden brewhouse to a mostly brick complex of fourteen buildings including refrigerated storehouses, a stable for horse-drawn delivery wagons, and, according to legend, a beer-dispensing spigot on one outdoor wall.

In 1895, Rudolph's oldest son, Rudolph Jr., moved to Fall River to start the Old Colony Brewery, one of three in the booming textile manufacturing city. He had studied chemistry at the Boston Institute of Technology—which later moved to Cambridge and became MIT—and attended the United States Brewer's Academy in New York City. In 1910, Old Colony acquired the other two Fall River breweries, Enterprise Brewing and King Philip Brewing, thus cementing the reputation of the Haffenreffers as shrewd businessmen. Kid brother Adolph took over the Fall River conglomerate after Prohibition, renaming it the Enterprise Brewing Co. and producing Boh, Old Tap, White Seal, and other brands until the mid-1950s.

During Prohibition, Haffenreffer & Co. purchased the rights to the Harvard Brewing Co. of Lowell's Pickwick Ale, named for the portly title character in Charles Dickens' *Pickwick Papers*. Harvard was one of the biggest breweries in New England before Prohibition and immediately afterward. However, during World War II, one of its employees was arrested for spying for the Germans. Not only that, German stockholders had a controlling interest in the enterprise. Concerned that Harvard profits may have been funding the enemy, the feds seized the company and held it until the 1950s. The ordeal put a damper on business, to say the least, and the brewery shut down in 1956.

Meanwhile, Haffenreffer & Co. was going strong with Pickwick. It had produced the beverage as Pickwick Pale, a near beer, during the dry years. After Repeal, with another of Rudolph's sons, Theodore, at the helm, the alcoholic version returned to the market. Stronger than the light lagers that dominated most of the country, Pickwick Ale was a sort of precursor to Private Stock; its nickname was "poor man's whiskey." In 1999, the Harpoon Brewery revived Pickwick Ale yet again, but only briefly. Maybe its reputation was just a little too gritty for the aspirational craft beer drinker.

Today, what remains of the Haffenreffer & Co. brewery complex is on the register of historic places and is an economic development zone anchored by the Boston Beer Company's pilot brewery—a popular tourist attraction that features a museum about Hub brewing history and a tasting room where you can sample the many flavors of Sam Adams. You know you're near the place when you see what's left of a smokestack reading "FENREFFER BEER."

In 2009, two of Rudolph Haffenreffer's descendants, Peter Haffenreffer and Nick Shields, reacquired the rights to Private Stock from Pabst, which had kept the malt liquor wheezing along. "It's a shadow of its former self," says Shields, who has a master's degree in food science from Cornell University. He and his cousin moved production of P-Stock to the Latrobe brewery in Pennsylvania and the F.X. Matt

Before he became "Dr. Seuss," Theodor Geisel drew advertisements for Narragansett, courtesy of Narragansett Beer.

brewery in New York, and they lowered the alcohol content to 6 percent to enter certain states' markets more easily. Stuck at an unprofitably low price and competing with the other malt liquors that have sprung up since Private Stock's gangsta heyday, the Haffenreffers' second-most famous beer may have lived its last life, acknowledges Shields. He is considering the possibility of bringing back an old recipe or two from the pre-Prohibition Haffenreffer & Co.—beers that would compete in the craft segment. Shields chuckles that his grandfather, Theodore C. Haffenreffer Jr., the owner of the Jamaica Plain brewery when it closed in 1964, wouldn't be impressed with the idea. "He kept wanting to predict that the craft brewing movement wouldn't come to much."

———◇———

Now for the story of the Haffenreffer family's best-known beer. The Narragansett Brewing Co. was built in 1890 by a group of German-

Americans that included Jacob Wirth, founder of the famous Boston saloon on Stuart Street that is still serving beer today. In 1931, when Repeal looked imminent, Narragansett's shareholders approached Rudolph Haffenreffer Jr. for help financing and managing the modernization of the brewery. He agreed and apparently liked the company so much that he became president and chairman.

Rudolph knew that the brewery's future depended on marketing. He hired a Dartmouth classmate of his sons named Theodor Geisel—the future Dr. Seuss—to create company icon Chief 'Gansett, a cigar-store Indian that appeared on beer trays, posters, and other promotional items. Advertising manager Jack Haley coined the slogan "Hi Neighbor—have a 'Gansett," which Red Sox radio announcer Curt Gowdy broadcast all over the Northeast on behalf of the team's official sponsor. (The Sox-Narragansett partnership lasted from 1946 to 1975.) And, of course, there was a "Hi Neighbor Girl," Irene Hennessy.

Narrangansett's marketing leaned highbrow as well. The brewery sponsored the just-launched Newport Jazz Festival in 1954 and the legendary Dylan-goes-electric Newport Folk Festival of 1965. Animated TV ads featured the voices of urbane comic duo Elaine May and Mike Nichols, who would go on to direct *The Graduate* and other classic movies. No other New England brewer advertised as broadly and relentlessly as 'Gansett did.

By 1955, Narragansett was New England's best-selling beer, with a 65 percent share of the market. Its flagship was the lager, but it also brewed ale, porter, bock, and other styles in addition to the Croft and Hanley brands it acquired. In 1959, the brewery achieved its first-ever annual output of one million barrels. Every bottle and can of 'Gansett declared that the contents within were "Made on honor, sold on merit."

And then came the 1960s.

During this decade, the brewing industry was like that cartoon of a fish about to be swallowed by a bigger fish about to be swal-

Courtesy of Narragansett Beer.

lowed by a bigger fish, and so on. Narragansett was the big fish in New England, buying out other breweries in the region. In 1964, at the height of Narragansett's success, the Haffenreffers in Cranston bought out their cousins at Haffenreffer & Co. in Boston (the deal was friendly) and agreed to produce its brands, including Pickwick and Private Stock. The next year, a bigger fish from the Midwest came along and—gulp—the Haffenreffer family exited the beer business after one hundred years as brewers.

The bigger fish was Falstaff. The St. Louis-based brewery had itself been on a frenzied mission to bulk up through acquisitions. Its plan was to bring its own flagship beer to New England and distribute Narrangansett nationwide. But consumers, especially younger ones, weren't enthusiastic. Falstaff and 'Gansett were their granddads' brews. They wanted Schlitz, Bud, and other big national brands.

In 1970, Anheuser-Busch built a mammoth new plant in Merrimack, New Hampshire that made Narragansett's circa-1890 brewery look rinky-dink. Not only could the St. Louis behemoth get more product out to more customers, it had the means to offer attractive incentives to bar owners, according to Bill Anderson, who started out as an apprentice at Narragansett and worked his way up to brewmaster. As he remembers it, "We'd put up a lamp. Anheuser-Busch would put in a pool table."

Anderson was brewmaster from 1967 to 1975, after Falstaff had taken over and added New York's Ballantine Ale to Narragansett's emporium of dying brands. The new owners "bit off more than they could chew," he says. "They weren't brewers. They were just looking for paychecks." Amazingly, the Cranston brewery hung on until 1983. It was demolished in 1998.

In 2005, Mark Hellendrung, a former executive of Nantucket Nectars and consultant for the Magic Hat brewery in Vermont, organized a group of investors to buy the rights to Narragansett back from Falstaff, which had continued to brew ever-dwindling amounts in Indiana and Wisconsin. He then set about reviving this "legacy" brand, which is how people in the beverage business refer to forgotten megabrews from back in the day. The most famous legacy brand is Pabst Blue Ribbon, which made a spectacular comeback in the 1990s at bars frequented by bike messengers, musicians, and other hip drinkers shunning brands they perceived as too corporate. A Rhode Island native, Hellendrung bet that a combination of regional nostalgia, retro coolness, and demand for local products would put Narragansett Lager back on New England's map.

The beer isn't actually locally produced; it's brewed at the Rochester, New York branch of North American Breweries from a recipe that Bill Anderson himself helped recreate. It's much easier, of course, to make beer at an existing brewery than to build your own, although Hellendrung's eventual goal is to locate production in New England. He hired Providence craft brewer Sean Larkin of the Trinity Brewhouse and Revival Brewing Co. to formulate most of Narragansett's seasonal and other specialty beers, inspired by styles that were once brewed in Cranston: porter, bock, cream ale, fest lager, and summer ale (based on the old Narragansett Banquet Ale), among others. While the flagship beer, like other legacy brands, is a cheap, corn-based light lager, the other offerings are all or mostly malt beers (and are priced accordingly). The cool thing is, the fancier beers come in tallboy cans with bright colors and bold lettering, just like 'Gansett lager.

In the past few years, craft brewers have embraced cans like a respectable family reclaims a black sheep who grows up to be a rock star. Harpoon installed a canning line in its Boston brewery that it proudly shows off behind a glass wall running the length of a spacious new beer hall. The New England Brewing Co. in Connecticut, the Newburyport and Wachusett breweries in Massachusetts, and the Baxter Brewing Co. in Maine have all bet big on cans. The Alchemist Brewery in Waterbury, Vermont, which produces a single beer—Heady Topper, a double IPA that is one of the most sought-after brews in America—packages its product in shiny, silver tallboys. And the big kahuna of craft beer, Boston Beer Company, spent two years and more than one million dollars developing a special can that delivers a Jim Koch-approved sensory experience. It was released in spring 2013, in time for can-friendly outdoor activities like boating, golfing, and camping.

The megabrewers have known how sensible cans are for decades, which is precisely why the containers carried such a stigma in the craft brewing world. Handcrafted beer simply did not come in cans. It was more expensive to make than mass-market brews and had to be priced higher, like an import. It had to come in a bottle, because who was going to spend eight or ten dollars on a six-pack of cans? And there was the lingering notion that beer in cans tasted metallic. That may have been true in the 1970s, but the technology has come a long way. Beer in cans tastes just fine.

It took a few pioneering craft brewers to just go ahead and put their beer in cans and show consumers there was nothing to be afraid of. The Oskar Blues brewery in Colorado was first, releasing Dale's Pale Ale in cans in 2002 when it was still but a wee brewpub. Now it's one of the top fifty craft brewers in the United States.

Another trailblazer was the New England Brewing Co. in Woodbridge, Connecticut (a few miles outside of New Haven), which began canning in 2003. Owned by veteran brewer Rob Leonard, who worked in the 1990s for the New Haven Brewing Co. and the John Harvards's brewpub chain, it is the second incarnation of one of the region's earliest craft breweries. Leonard and his partner Matt Westfall ditched the earlier company's staid, bottled flagship, Atlantic Amber, and began making rowdy canned beers like Sea Hag IPA, 668 The Neighbor of the Beast (a Belgian-style strong pale ale), and Ghandi-Bot, a double IPA whose logo is, yes, a robotic version of the prophet (remember that IPA stands for *India pale ale*). Sales have climbed ever since.

The small breweries that pioneered craft canning did it, as with everything else, by hand. Astonishingly, New England Brewing relied on a small, table-top apparatus that canned one beer at a time before the recent installation of automated equipment. "I guess a lot of people thought I was crazy," Leonard said of his decision to can beer when hardly anyone else was doing it. "Now there are cans everywhere."

Yes, cans. They're hot all of a sudden. Now you can be at, say, an outdoor concert and enjoy craft beer in a container that won't shatter during the acoustic guitar solo. Plus, just as brewers back in 1935 understood, cans benefit the flavor of beer by blocking light and leaving very little room for air. They come with their own label and have a smaller impact on the environment than bottles. Oh, and a woman can carry a six-pack of them out of the store all by herself.

Flask A   Flask B

Glucose and
Yeast solution   Gas bubbles

Yeast

Without yeast, there would be no beer. The same microorganism that makes bread rise turns the natural sugars found in malted barley, grapes, and other plants into ethanol and carbon dioxide—booze and bubbles. In winemaking, the bubbles are allowed to escape the fermenting liquid, unless you're making a sparkling wine.

There are different strains of yeast used to make British ales, American ales, German lagers, and Belgian ales, to name only a few broad categories of beer. To make a Bavarian-style hefeweizen (wheat beer), for example, you could use a yeast strain that accentuates one of two dominant flavor characteristics—banana or clove—or one that fairly balances the two. Brewers of a Belgian sour ale called lambic let wild yeast in the air ferment their beer. Like cliff diving, this primitive method of beermaking is marveled at but rarely imitated. Most brewers start out with a pure yeast strain propagated in a lab. The yeast regenerates with each batch of beer and forms a shaving cream-like slurry that brewers pitch into the next batch to ferment.

For most of human history, the fact that this slurry was composed of trillions of sugar-eating, alcohol-excreting microscopic organisms was unknown. Fermentation was considered a miracle. Even we modern people who know about microbiology can be impressed by the phenomenon. If you've ever watched a bread dough rise or a batch of beer bubble and foam, you've probably thought to yourself, if only fleetingly, "Hmm, fermentation *is* kind of a miracle."

The craft beer revolution itself was kind of a miracle. When it took off in the early 1980s, there were only 40-odd brewing companies left in a country of 227 million people following decades in which big breweries kept getting bigger. Those companies were all essentially making the same beer: American-style pilsner, or light lager. Heavy on adjunct grains (corn or rice instead of barley), light on hops, and artificially carbonated, American beer was seemingly swilled contentedly by a public that had forsaken the robust ales, porters, bocks, and amber lagers of the industrial past.

In that "one beer to rule them all" environment, the first craft brewers were rebels. Like Eastern Bloc DJs sneaking Motown records onto the airwaves during the Cold War, they introduced all-malt, amply hopped, richly colored beers to the few drinkers adventurous enough to appreciate them. They led a revolution that freed beer from the industrial fortress and brought it back to the kitchen and the small brewery, where people could make it themselves or at least watch it being made and taste it fresh out of the tank. Unlike the megabrewers, who kept their wan formulations under wraps, most small-scale brewers gladly shared their recipes and techniques with peers and consumers. They had to. It was as much about gaining badly needed professional expertise as educating the public about what the hell this "dark beer" was.

The seeds of this particular revolution were planted in San Francisco, 1965. That's when Fritz Maytag (of the family that brought us the washing machines and the blue cheese) rescued the Anchor Steam Brewery from extinction. Anchor was one of America's last surviving regional breweries from the Industrial Age, and the "steam beer" it produced—an amber lager fermented at a warm temperature like an ale—is the only style of beer native to the United States. The other key dateline is also in California: Sonoma, 1976. That's when Bill McAuliffe, a former naval nuclear submarine mechanic who learned to homebrew while stationed in Scotland, started the first new American brewery since Prohibition and called it New Albion.

Those two pioneers faced ridiculous odds. Maytag was able to tap his family's fortune during the ten years it took Anchor to turn a profit. McAuliffe, on the other hand, had little capital. He worked insane hours trying to keep up with demand for his New Albion Pale Ale yet never became profitable enough to expand. That predicament, which bedevils many startup breweries to this day, forced him to shut down in 1982. Nevertheless, McAuliffe, along with Maytag, inspired new waves of like-minded entrepreneurs, some of whom, like Ken Grossman and Paul Camusi of Sierra Nevada and Jim Koch of Boston Beer, went on to transform the industry.

That the first New England craft breweries didn't emerge until a decade after New Albion opened is the evidence upon which smug West Coasters accuse us of arriving laughably late to the party. In reality, New England exerted a typically under-the-radar influence much earlier than that, cultivating future craft beer makers and their fans. Homebrewers led the way.

———◆———

Pat Baker didn't know he was fomenting a quiet revolution when he started a mail-order business of home winemaking and brewing equipment out of his basement in Westport, Connecticut in 1968. A Yale graduate of chemistry, he had been making wine out of grapes he had planted to disguise a drab fence in his yard. There were already a few purveyors of winemaking supplies in the United States at that time, but homebrewing supplies had to be imported from England largely because making beer for private consumption was still illegal in America. *Huh?* Yeah, funny thing: after Prohibition, a law was written to re-legalize both home winemaking and homebrewing, but the words "and/or beer" were mistakenly lopped off the page. This is why the world needs proofreaders.

The mistake was finally corrected in 1979, thanks in part to Baker's bridge-partner-turned-business-partner, Nancy Crosby, who came aboard in 1972. As Crosby & Baker, they ran what became one of the largest beer and winemaking supply houses in the country. They had the mail-order business and a retail shop. More important, they started a wholesale operation that outfitted other retailers across the country. Later on, they added commercial craft brewers to their clien-

Pat Baker in the late 1960s, courtesy of Pat Baker and Nancy Crosby.

tele. (They sold the business in 1989, and it was acquired in 2011 by Beverage Supply Group, which renamed it BSG HandCraft.)

Crosby, who had worked in a bookstore and dreamed of being a business owner, ran the company day to day. Baker, who worked for the industrial chemical company Olin Corp., came in on Saturdays and would often end up giving informal how-to clinics for customers. "I was sort of a beer doctor," Baker says, adding, "I was less dumb than everybody else."

In those days, reliable information about homebrewing was rare. Recipes, often relics of the Prohibition era, called for a sizable quantity of sugar in addition to malt syrup. Sugar doesn't do much for a beer's flavor, but it boosts the alcohol content, which was priority number-one for homebrewers during the dry years. The only hops available were often so stale they were like little pellets of cardboard. And to turn these ingredients into beer, many people used dried baker's yeast, which was readily available but hit-or-miss when it came to fermenting malt beverages. Baker eventually wrote and self-published *The New Brewer's Handbook* (1984), which was both an accessible how-to guide for homebrewers and an effective marketing tool.

Who was shopping for homebrew supplies at Crosby & Baker in the 1970s? Scientist-tinkerers like Baker. Bikers and other counterculture types. People who had traveled to Europe and wanted to recreate the flavorful beers they'd tried there. And frugal folk who were pleased to discover that they could easily make beer at home for significantly less than the cost of store-bought beer. Avid brewers would so often congregate at Crosby & Baker and exchange tips that Baker started a homebrew club called the Underground Brewers in 1975. The club is still going and is the oldest such organization in the country after the Maltose Falcons, which began in Los Angeles in 1974.

The Underground Brewers were initially just that, practicing their illegal hobby discreetly. Or not. Baker's attitude toward the feds was, "Come get me. I'd love to argue about it." That never happened. Instead, he and Crosby launched the Home Wine and Beer Trade

Association (HWBTA) in 1974 as an umbrella for the nation's rogue wine shops that sold homebrew supplies. Under Crosby's leadership, the HWBTA joined forces with the American Homebrewers Association, which started in Colorado in 1978, and Lee Coe, a homebrewing instructor and member of the Maltose Falcons, to lobby Congress to change the silly law that let people make wine in their homes but not beer. They got the attention of U.S. Senator Alan Cranston, who had a homebrewer on his staff and represented California, a state that had already spawned a fledgling industry of small brewers. He was instrumental in the legislation's passage, and Jimmy Carter signed HR 1337 into law in October 1978, making homebrewing legal as of February 1, 1979. The *MacNeil-Lehrer NewsHour* filmed a short segment on the triumph at Crosby & Baker, which had moved from Westport, Connecticut, to Westport, Massachusetts. "It was our minute and a half of fame," Crosby quips.

The legalization of homebrewing may have been a blip on the national news, but for the future of craft beer, it was huge. "Legalization at the federal level had opened up the pipeline for higher-quality ingredients and now allowed for a freer flow of ideas between commercial brewers and the homebrewers who might want to join them," writes Tom Acitelli in his history of the craft-beer revolution, *The Audacity of Hops* (2013). Many if not most commercial craft brewers have homebrewed at some point in their lives.

In the 1980s, other homebrew clubs sprang up in New England alongside Connecticut's Underground Brewers, most notably the Wort Processors of greater Boston. There were also the Valley Fermenters of western Massachusetts, the Green Mountain Mashers of Vermont, and the Maine Ale and Lager Tasters (a.k.a. M.A.L.T.). New Hampshire's Brew Free or Die launched in 1991.

Members of these clubs entered local, regional, and national competitions in which anywhere from a couple dozen to several hundred people vied in blind tastings for titles like Best of Class and Best of Show. Some of the prizewinners went pro. Phil Markowski and Ron

Page of the Underground Brewers landed at the New England Brewing Co., which opened in Norwalk, Connecticut, in 1990. Markowski gained national recognition at the Southampton Publick House in New York and is now a partner at the cutting-edge Two Roads Brewery in Stratford, Connecticut. Page has for many years made well-crafted beers at the City Steam Brewery Café in Hartford.

From the Wort Processors, Tod Mott created Harpoon's popular IPA and one of the country's most sought-after beers, the Portsmouth Brewery's Kate the Great Imperial Stout. His fellow club member Darryl Goss put the Cambridge Brewing Co. in Massachusetts on the map in the 1990s by, for example, brewing Tripel Threat, the country's first commercial Belgian-style beer. (Darryl lost a valiant battle with ALS in 2012.)

Steve Stroud, a founding member of the Wort Processors and a

Tod Mott during his Porstmouth Brewery days, late 2000s, courtesy of Tod Mott.

multi-award winner himself, says of these guys, "You knew when you tasted their beers back in 1984 that they knew how to brew. You knew even back then."

Stroud was instrumental in helping Baker bring legitimacy to homebrew competitions. In the early days of these events, skeptics of anything outside of mainstream beer snickered at the credentials (and sobriety) of the self-proclaimed judges who were awarding these titles. Who did they think they were? They were, in fact, the first beer geeks. With Baker, Stroud, and Betty Ann Sather (who would later marry Baker) leading the way, and with the British beer writer Michael Jackson's *World Guide to Beer* (1977) for inspiration, they catalogued the characteristics of dozens of beer styles so that homebrews could be judged in their proper categories—stouts with stouts, pilsners with pilsners, Belgian saisons with Belgian saisons, etc.

In 1985, they devised a rigorous exam for prospective beer judges, based on the style guidelines they had written up, that became the national Beer Judge Certification Program (BJCP). With Baker at the helm and with support from the American Homebrewers Association, the program certified two thousand judges in its first decade. Major competitions such as the Great American Beer Festival, the World Beer Cup, and the National Homebrew Competition recruit BJCP judges and base beer evaluation on the program's guidelines.

Just like wine, craft beer demanded its own vocabulary and professional evaluators. The fact that you're not laughing at that notion owes a lot to people like Baker and his fellow beer geeks. They were passionate about what Baker calls "real beer," and they wanted people to take it seriously.

———◆———

According to Baker, Jim Koch said he made his first batch of homebrew with supplies he bought at the Crosby & Baker store in Westport, Massachusetts. That batch was the beginning of a mission, begun in the early 1980s, to turn Koch's great-great-grandfather's recipe for a copper-colored brew called Vienna lager into a quality American-made beer that could compete with imports.

Fast-forward thirty years: Boston Beer Company is the fifth-largest brewer, and the largest craft brewer, in the United States. Samuel Adams is for sale in all fifty states, Canada, Mexico, and some parts of Europe and Asia. You can find it at the convenience store and the fine restaurant, the stadium and the airport. The vast majority of Sam Adams is made and sold outside New England. More than any other craft beer, it's a national brand.

Yet the beer was born in Boston. Its headquarters are there, and so is its pilot brewery in the old Haffenreffer plant in Jamaica Plain. The man whom we've all seen in TV ads rubbing aromatic

Jim Koch at a 2012 tasting of his rare barrel-aged beer Utopias, courtesy of Terry Lozoff.

hop flowers between his palms came to the area from Cincinnati in the late 1960s to major in government at Harvard. He was the first elder son in generations to veer from the family vocation of brewing. That was a relief to his father, Charles, for whom memories of big breweries eating little breweries for lunch were still fresh.

Jim was a high achiever. He stayed on at Harvard to earn an MBA and a law degree, was an instructor for Outward Bound, and then embarked on a career as a management consultant for the Boston Consulting Group. He worked alongside future corporate titans such as Jeffrey Immelt of General Electric and Mitt Romney, who would go on to fame as the head of Bain Capital, the governor of Massachusetts, and the 2012 Republican presidential candidate.

On paper, the future looked bright. But Koch wasn't feeling it. "I just wasn't comfortable with the big company culture, bureaucracy, and politics. I wanted to stand on my own two feet and accomplishments rather than succeed in an organizational context. I quickly settled on beer. It was like destiny," Koch told *Fortune* magazine. It's ironic that what today's hardcore beer enthusiasts consider the most corporate of craft beer companies started out as an escape from corporate culture.

While still at BCG in the early 1980s, Koch read about Fritz Maytag and tasted microbrews on business trips out West. The takeaway from his travels was as much cautionary as inspirational. He observed New Albion's financial downfall and tasted some pretty bad beer by startups fueled more by passion than brewing ability. Sierra Nevada of Chico, California, and Anchor Steam were solid, he says, but "Redhook [Ale of Seattle] was infected, Cartwright [of Portland, Oregon] was not very good, Boulder [Brewing Company of Colorado] had terrible sanitation problems. I thought, 'I've got to find a better way to do this.'"

He made two key decisions. He hired the nation's premier beer biochemist, Joseph Owades, to help formulate a brew based on that old recipe from his ancestor's eponymous Louis Koch Brewery in St.

Louis. Owades, the inventor of light beer, had previously consulted for Anchor and the New Amsterdam Brewing Company, which produced New York's first bottled craft beer.

On his father's advice, Koch also contracted with the Pittsburgh Brewing Company in Pennsylvania, which had been around since the 1860s, to brew his beer rather than spend millions building his own facility in Massachusetts. The elder Koch knew from hard experience that there were plenty of existing breweries with excess capacity and quality control. Why not rent their equipment and expertise?

Before it was a widely adopted practice, contract brewing incited controversy among craft brewers. Koch just wanted to make consistent, quality beer and have a decent shot at turning a profit sooner rather than later. When he and Owades determined that the flavor of their product—a malty, copper-colored lager with spicy German hops and a luxuriant head—was exactly where they wanted it, and that it could be reproduced cleanly and consistently, it was time to start putting Samuel Adams Boston Lager in front of discerning beer drinkers.

Koch brought twenty-three-year-old Rhonda Kallman on as a partner. She was a BCG secretary from Peabody, Massachusetts, who moonlighted as a bartender and excelled at sales. Distributors, beholden to the megabrewers, wouldn't touch the unknown brand, so Koch and Kallman sold the first few hundred cases out of a rented truck while still working for BCG. Bars and restaurants in the Boston area, including one of Koch's favorite old pubs, Doyle's in Jamaica Plain, signed on pretty quickly. Acitelli writes that Koch and Kallman knew "that if they could get the beer in the glass in front of a manager or an owner, they could get the account." Sam Adams had the bold flavor and upscale packaging that import drinkers sought, but it was better made than most imports (which were often brewed with adjuncts for the American market), and it was fresh. The whole concept was mind-blowing in 1985.

Most early New England craft brewers had an experience much different from Koch's. They lacked his financial resources, business acumen, and industry connections. In fact, they were kind of like the very first New England brewers, the ones who arrived in the 1600s, in that they were hard-pressed for equipment, ingredients, know-how, and capital. Like their forebears, they had to be resourceful. They repurposed old factories, warehouses, and restaurants. They scavenged dairy tanks and soda bottling machinery. They used wooden boat oars to mash in (stir malt with hot water) and pantyhose stuffed with hop pellets to flavor a conditioning tank full of beer. They custom-built grain mills, fermenting vessels, and keg washers. And while they were cobbling together their breweries,

David Geary, courtesy of the D. L. Geary Brewing Company.

they lobbied their state legislatures to declare these ventures legal.

That's right—the small brewer was up against the legacy of the three-tier system for the manufacture and sale of alcohol, established after Prohibition. Because beer and liquor producers had been partly responsible for the proliferation of saloons in the late 1800s and early 1900s, they were banned from selling directly to the bar owner or the consumer; they had to go through a middleman, the distributor. But distribution in the late twentieth century was all about volume. Very few wholesalers thought it worthwhile to tack a few cases of an unknown brand onto their Bud, Miller, and Coors-dominated portfolios. In order to bring their product to market, microbrewers would have to distribute it themselves. Brewpubs, in which beer was made and served in the same building (a perfectly natural concept for most of human history), similarly thwarted the middle tier. So, just as Congress in the 1970s heard from homebrewers who wanted their hobby legalized, state lawmakers in the 1980s had to be convinced that it was reasonable for a brewer producing a small amount of beer to sell it directly to retailers and consumers.

Luckily, David "D. L." Geary of Portland, Maine, who opened the first microbrewery east of the Rockies, had an ally in State Representative Henry Cabot. Cabot, who owned a pub in Waldoboro, championed legislation in 1985 that permitted small Maine breweries to self-distribute and/or to brew and serve on-premises.

Geary, a Purdue engineering alumnus who worked for a medical-supply company, hatched his brewery idea over pints at Three Dollar Dewey's Ale House on Commercial Street in Portland. Dewey's, which opened in 1981, was a mecca for people who liked good beer and the atmosphere of an authentic British pub—no TV, communal seating, newspapers strewn about. There were few, if any, bars like it in New England at the time. (Its name is a sly joke, reportedly taken from a "menu" that prostitutes who followed gold miners to the Klondike presented to their customers: $1 Lookie, $2 Feelie, $3 Dewey.)

Deweys' owner, Alan Eames, was a pure New England character.

He would later find celebrity as the self-styled "Indiana Jones of beer," who scoured Egyptian tombs and observed primitive brewing rites in South America for evidence of the role beer played in ancient and traditional societies. He wrote several books on the topic, gave lectures, and made media appearances. His colorful storytelling and self-promotion made some view him as more huckster than scholar, but there's no denying that he did much to spread the word about the cultural and nutritional importance of beer throughout history. *The New York Times* ran an obituary of Eames when he died unexpectedly of respiratory failure in 2007 at age fifty-nine.

Before he turned the world on to beer and civilization, Eames turned New Englanders on to civilized beer. He rejected major American brands in favor of imports, a radical move akin to flag burning in those days. And we're not talking anything as pedestrian as Heineken; we're talking Guinness Stout, Whitbread Ale, and Traquair House Ale. The latter is a strong, dark, malty beer called a "wee heavy," and it is made in a 350-year-old brewery inside a Scottish castle. "That beer was a revelation to me," says Geary.

"Back then, almost all the good beers were imports," he told a Vermont newspaper in 2012. "We barely knew about the microbreweries out West ... and we couldn't get any of the beers anyway."

It's no exaggeration to say that the early years of New England craft brewing were influenced more by what was happening on the other side of the Atlantic than what was happening on the other side of America.

Eames was all for Geary's plan to make traditional ales commercially in Maine. One day the publican introduced his friend to a customer in town from Scotland: Peter Maxwell Stuart, the Laird of Traquair House, where Geary's favorite beer was brewed. When Geary incorporated the D. L. Geary Brewing Company in 1983, the laird helped the American secure apprenticeships at several British breweries, including Traquair House. With his wife, Karen, remaining in Portland to write a business plan, Geary left for Great Britain to learn how to brew. That's where he met bio-chemist-turned-brewer Alan Pugsley, who would work for Geary and later compete with him.

Pugsley was the young right-hand man of Peter Austin, who owned England's first modern-day microbrewery, Ringwood in Hampshire County. It was one of the places where Geary served as an apprentice, and he and Pugsley hit it off. Part of Austin's business was selling brewing systems to small startup breweries all over the world that wanted to make English ales. "In 1986, the USA was as desolate as China or Africa in regards to brewery suppliers," declares Pugsley, who actually traveled to China and Africa to establish Austin breweries.

Once Geary returned to the States, and he and Karen had scrounged enough investment from family and friends to build a brewery in an industrial park on the outskirts of Portland, he called on Pugsley. The gangly Englishman helped Geary set up an Austin brewhouse and formulated the flagship Geary's Pale Ale. It was just the beer D. L. had hoped for—dry and crisp with a hint of fruiti-ness and hitting a fine balance between malt and hops. It was a New World version of a classic British pale ale, but, unlike an import, it would still be fresh when it filled New Englanders' beer mugs. After three years of business plan writing, fundraising, apprenticing, and legal paperwork, kegs of Geary's Pale Ale were finally ready for delivery in December 1986. The first keg was tapped, of course, at Three Dollar Dewey's.

When his contract with Geary's was up, Pugsley went on to help launch several other breweries on the East Coast, including Gritty McDuff's brewpub in Portland, Tremont in Charlestown, Massa-chusetts, and Magic Hat in Burlington, Vermont. Finally, he start-ed his own brewery, Shipyard in Portland, in 1994. He has been one of New England's most prominent names in craft beer as well as one of its most controversial. That controversy has to do with yeast, actually. Like Geary's, all of Pugsley's subsequent startups used a yeast strain that originated at the Ringwood Brewery in England. Some brewers admire the strain because it ferments vigorously and can produce pleasant esters (fruity flavors) and a dry finish that accentuates hop character.

The Great Ringwood Invasion might have been consequential to only one man: D. L. Geary. He was none too pleased when all these breweries started sprouting up, producing Ringwood-fermented English-style beers that were competitive siblings of Geary's Pale Ale.

But he was not alone in his chagrin. With anything that becomes ubiquitous and successful, there is a backlash. Bashers of Ringwood yeast complain of its tendency to produce beers with a buttery aroma. While a hint of this characteristic, which brewers call diacetyl, is appropriate for some British ales, too much of it is just gross. Ringwood beers acquired a reputation as butter bombs, and some brewers who used the yeast downplayed that fact while their peers opening newer breweries deliberately shunned it.

The whole thing got silly. Diacetyl is hardly exclusive to Ringwood yeast. Many beers fermented with other strains can suffer from an overabundance of diacetyl. And some beers fermented with Ring-

Will Meyers mashing in, courtesy of Cambridge Brewing Company.

wood have no discernable butteriness—Geary's Pale Ale being one example. Geary and Pugsley both point out that not only can a careful brewer control the expression of diacetyl, but with each successive fermentation, new generations of Ringwood yeast develop a unique house character. "Geary's yeast is Geary's yeast, and Shipyard's yeast is Shipyard's yeast," Pugsley says.

———◇———

The British influence on New England beer was also obvious in the region's first brewpub, which opened in Boston six months before the first kegs of Geary's hit the market. The Commonwealth Brewing Co. was the brainchild of Manchester, England native Richard Wrigley, who had opened the Manhattan Brewing Company a year earlier. His partners in Boston were Jeff and Jim Lee, Chinese-American brothers who knew the restaurant business.

The Commonwealth was a marquee establishment. Through large plate-glass windows, passers-by could see a spacious restaurant with wooden floors, copper-topped tables, brass railings, and shiny copper kettles (those were for show—the not-so-shiny copper kettle in which the beer was actually brewed was in an adjacent room). Wrigley asked Derrick Hobson, former brewmaster at the Bass Brewery in Burton-on-Trent, England, to help formulate the beer recipes and train brewer Phil Leinhart, who landed at the Commonwealth right out of college, where he majored in chemistry. In the brewpub's basement, special bitter, stout, and old ale fermented in custom-built "Yorkshire squares"—actual square-shaped vats—and aged in grundies, or tanks that look like cartoon submarines, shipped over from England. Celtics and Bruins fans en route to nearby Boston Garden, flight crews from British Airways and other visiting Brits, and a small band of local beer enthusiasts made up the bulk of the clientele.

Customers who didn't fall into the latter two groups faced a steep learning curve, because all of the Commonwealth's beer, at first, was barely carbonated and served at cellar temperature. *What?* Yes, it's called cask-conditioned ale. We Yanks used to dismiss it as warm and flat. "We were ahead of our time," says Jim Lee. After losing a few thousand dollars on buybacks of pints from disgruntled customers, the brewery began chilling and boosting the carbonation of some of its beer. "That bridged the gap for a while," Lee says. "But what we saw was that people's palates adjusted, and they started to appreciate what we did."

Many craft beer drinkers in New England today are unaware of the Commonwealth, which closed in 2002 in the aftermath of the first explosion of craft breweries. But they have probably tasted its legacy. In the 1980s and 1990s, when a new brewery seemed to open up every five minutes, the Commonwealth served as a sort of teaching hospital for New England brewers.

Among the notable alums of the Portland Street brewpub are Leinhart, who went on to work for Anheuser-Busch and is now brewmaster at Ommegang in Cooperstown, New York; John Mallet, brewmaster at Bell's Brewery in Michigan; Steve Slesar, who launched the Boston Beer Works chain of brewpubs; Tim Morse, former director of brewing operations at the John Harvard's chain of brewpubs; Dan Kramer, who made his career in western Massachusetts and recently started the boutique Element Brewing Co. in Millers Falls; and Tod Mott, who has also worked at Harpoon and the Portsmouth Brewery.

Kramer, who started out at the Commonwealth as a busboy and eventually became head brewer, no doubt speaks for all of the above when he says: "I just wanted to be a part of it—any part of it. I just wanted to work there and be exposed to freshly made beer. It was a concept that never occurred to me was even possible. Breweries were these huge places that took up city blocks. Not a little restaurant in the middle of downtown Boston."

By 1990, nine more breweries had launched in New England alongside Boston Beer, Geary's, and the Commonwealth. The year 1987 brought us the Catamount Brewing Company in White River Junction, Vermont, the Massachusetts Bay Brewing Co., a.k.a. Harpoon, in Boston, and the Northampton Brewery in western Massachusetts. Two brewpubs, Gritty McDuff's in Portland and the Vermont Pub & Brewery in Burlington, Vermont, opened in 1988. The class of 1989 includes the Elm City Brewing Company in New Haven, the Long Trail Brewery in Bridgewater, Vermont, and the Cambridge Brewing Co. in Cambridge. Finally, 1990 introduced Connecticut's New England Brewing Company. New Hampshire's and Rhode Island's first craft breweries, the Portsmouth Brewery and Union Station Brewing, came along in 1991 and 1993, respectively.

Remarkably, most of those pioneering breweries are still thriving; only Catamount and Elm City are no longer with us. (The New England Brewing Company was reincarnated under new ownership in Woodbridge, Connecticut.) There is camaraderie among their personnel, even though they may not run into each other much anymore. When these enterprises were in the planning stages, their owners made pilgrimages to the breweries that preceded them. Most of the world still considered craft beer an absurd idea in the late 1980s, so it helped to actually stand next to somebody else's mash tun, breathe in the aroma of steaming grain and think, "I'm not the only one crazy enough to think this can work."

It did work. New England homebrewers and early craft brewers lit a fuse that exploded in the 1990s. They were directly or indirectly responsible for dozens of new breweries that opened in the six states during that decade and afterward. Things would get a little crazy and there would be a crash, with some unfortunate casualties. But mostly, more breweries meant more people drinking craft beer and more success for brewers.

"For the first ten years there were hardly any of us," says Jim Koch. "As a brewer, you know that when you do a fermentation, when you don't have enough yeast, the fermentation won't work. When I started, there weren't enough yeast cells—it was much harder. It's a lot more fun to have company."

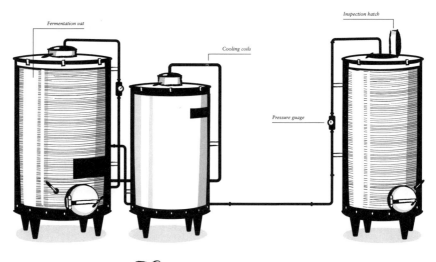

Fermentation vat
Inspection hatch
Cooling coils
Pressure guage

Fermentation

Fermentation is an amazing thing. To see it take place, tour a brewery that makes ales in open vessels (lagers are almost never made that way). In the early stages of fermentation, there doesn't seem to be much going on. When yeast is pitched into a batch of wort—malted barley extract that has been boiled with hops—it takes about twenty-four hours for the single-cell critters to multiply to the point where signs of their feasting on malt sugars materialize. Then it's party time. They form a thick, cappuccino-like foam of beige and tan on the surface of the liquid. It's like a circus tent under which you can hear lively bubbling. The yeast cells turn the malt sugars into alcohol and release carbon dioxide gas that, if you're standing in a room full of open fermenters, can make you lightheaded.

Within a few days, the yeast produce all the alcohol and CO_2 they can, and they are exhausted. Most go dormant until they're pitched into the next batch of wort. Some die. A few might mutate and start acting weird. Too many mutant yeast or other undesirable bacteria make for spoiled beer. It won't hurt you; it'll just smell strange, like bananas, buttered popcorn, egg salad, or band-aids. Most successful brewers avoid those pitfalls through religious devotion to sanitation and sound brewing methods.

In the 1980s, craft beer was in its early stages of fermentation; it was barely visible. In the 1990s, however, you couldn't miss it. The number of breweries in the United States grew from 120 in 1990 to more than 1,300 in 1998. If you lived in any decent-sized city or college town, you could get craft beer. It was party time.

One of the best ways for New England's fledgling brewers (most of whom had no formal training) to talk shop in those days was attending special banquets at Redbones BBQ in Somerville, Massachusetts. Owner Robert Gregory was one of the first Boston-area restaurateurs to embrace craft beer. He made a remarkable goodwill gesture toward those in the New England craft beer industry by regularly inviting them to Redbones for a free feast of ribs, pulled pork, and all the fixins'. Whatever local beers Gregory had on tap were supplemented with freshly bottled or kegged samples that attendees brought in. Brewers in Carhartts and flannel shirts stood around the bar animatedly talking shop. Camaraderie, insider knowledge, free barbecue, and a riot of beer—what fun!

There was the sense of being a part of something new, a shift in taste. The mainstream news referred to microbrews as a fad, but brewers knew better. First, some genuinely great beers had emerged, and a very small but enthusiastic group of people was clamoring for them. Second, a context for craft beer had already been established in the 1970s and 1980s. Artisanal cheeses and coffees, wines from small West Coast vintners, local produce sold at farmers' markets, and all manner of ethnic cuisines had greatly expanded the American palate.

The nation was growing increasingly curious about all things gastronomic. As David Kamp writes in his witty 2006 food history

The United States of Arugula: How We Became a Gourmet Nation, "Culinary sophistication is no longer the province of a tiny gourmet elite. The historically unrivaled run of prosperity in the United States in the eighties and nineties, compounded by the culinary advances [of the sixties and seventies], has led to the creation of an expanded leisure class that treats food as a cultural pastime, something you can follow the way you follow sports or the movies." In the 1990s, beer joined food and wine as a cultural pastime.

Additionally, brewers and beer enthusiasts were helping to revive an industry that had been an essential part of New England life for centuries before it largely disappeared in the 1960s and 1970s. They saw no reason why everyone from Bangor to Bridgeport shouldn't once again have at least one hometown beer.

———◆———

After pioneers like the D.L. Geary Brewing Company and the Commonwealth Brewing Company laid the legal and logistical foundations in the 1980s, the New England craft brewing scene took off. New beers were coming out every day, and they seemed to sell themselves. Head brewers left for new startups, assistant brewers got promoted, and apprentices were hired on the spot. The region's first beer festival, the Boston Brewers Festival, launched in 1992 and provided an important networking opportunity for brewers and showcase for consumers.

As with all revolutions, there was the excitement and fellowship of a shared mission. Staff from one brewery would gather at another as much to cheer their colleagues on as to borrow kegs or lend sacks of malt. Homebrew clubs held meetings at brewpubs and got expert feedback from the professional in rubber boots who had probably been a member of the club not too long before. Monthly "brews-papers" such as *Yankee Brew News* and *Ale Street News*, both of which covered the brewing industry in the Northeast, didn't just educate—they evangelized. And two brothers from Massachusetts started what would become the world's biggest website devoted to beer, BeerAdvocate.com.

Passion and impulse were the foundation of many a brewing start-up in those days. Some pioneers freely admit that they had little idea what they were getting themselves into.

Peter Egelston, a Southern California native and ex-Brooklyn schoolteacher who dabbled in homebrewing, opened the Northampton Brewery in western Massachusetts in 1987 with his sister Janet and her boyfriend, Mark Metzger. Janet and Mark were jazzed by the brewpubs they had visited out West and thought Northampton was the perfect college town in which to launch a similar venture on the East Coast.

A legal struggle plagued the partners for the first few years. For reasons that are still not entirely clear, they were denied the farmer-brewer's license under which their predecessor, the Commonwealth Brewing Company in Boston, operated. They had to divide their business into separate entities: a pub owned by Metzger and a manufacturer of beer owned by the Egelston siblings. That arrangement presented a problem when Janet and Mark decided to marry, as their two businesses would essentially be united along with the newlyweds.

The state declared the whole enterprise "extralegal," says Janet. "It was hell at the time. We were teetering on the brink of being shut down." Their conundrum made the news—even the *National Enquirer* picked it up!—which prompted a state senator from Northampton to resolve the situation with a piece of legislation that Governor Mike Dukakis signed. "The fact that our street is called Brewster Court is kind of odd," Janet muses, "in that we were laying the groundwork for a lot of brewers who followed." (Brewster is an archaic term for a female brewer.)

Meanwhile, Peter was dealing with his own challenge. "I made this really big jump from being a casual homebrewer to being a professional brewer in a brewpub," he says. "That was kind of stressful.

But in those days, people were very forgiving of a lot of the mistakes we made. Thank god. You could never get away with that today."

Back then, craft beer consumers may have been curious, even enthusiastic. But few were savvy. The novelty of the beverage obscured the fact that it could be wildly inconsistent. Hell, inconsistency was part of the novelty!

Phil Bannatyne faced a learning curve similar to the Egelstons'. The Stratford, Connecticut native with a sandy beard and compact, jockey-like build had spent most of the 1980s running a balloon-delivery business in San Francisco, where he sampled West Coast microbrews and tried his hand at making beer at home. He remembers visiting the Triple Rock brewpub in Berkeley the day it opened. The place was packed. Bannatyne started imagining opening a similar place back home in New England. He cashed out of the balloon business and enrolled in a summer brewing course at the University of California, Davis. In 1989, he moved back to New England and opened a brewpub in Berkeley's progressive East Coast counterpart: Cambridge, Massachusetts.

The Cambridge Brewing Company was, like the Northampton Brewery, inspired more by the West Coast beer scene than the British "real ale" revival. Its Tall Tale Pale Ale emulated Sierra Nevada Pale Ale, with its bright, citrusy Northwest hops, rather than more balanced English styles.

Bannatyne's plan was to single-handedly produce a variety of great beer and run a successful restaurant. "Pretty early on it occurred to me that I couldn't do both," he says. "The beer wasn't very good. In my own defense, it's a learning curve, and I didn't have a whole lot of time to learn it." Like most other beer entrepreneurs at that time, he had never brewed on a commercial system. He got some guidance from Russ Heissner, a fellow UC Davis grad, who was working at the Harpoon Brewery in South Boston. Then Darryl Goss, a talented homebrewer and vintage-motorcycle mechanic with a mop of curly hair, showed up at the door. As head brewer, he elevated the quality of the beer and, says Bannatyne, introduced the "innovative stuff that we've always done here." A few years later, another creative guy, Will Meyers, came on board and has been head brewer since 1997.

The Green Mountain State's first brewpub arrived in 1988, when husband-and-wife business partners Greg and Nancy Noonan started the Vermont Pub & Brewery in Burlington after spending three years persuading the state legislature to legalize their venture.

"We had no idea what we were doing," recalls Nancy. "We opened on a Friday night—major mistake. The food was my area. It was chaos. We were putting in one-hundred-hour weeks. We didn't even recognize ourselves, we looked so awful." Nevertheless, she says she was content to exit her former career as, of all things, a substance-abuse counselor.

Luckily, Greg had already mastered the technical side of brewing. In 1986, the obsessive homebrewer had published *Brewing Lager Beer*, a detailed guide that is considered a classic among craft brew-

Greg Noonan, founder of the Vermont Pub & Brewery and author of Brewing Lager Beer, *courtesy of Jerome Noonan.*

ers. (It is somewhat unfortunately titled, as its scope goes beyond lagers to other beer styles and to brewing in general.) Charlie Papazian, president of the Brewers Association and author of the widely read *Complete Joy of Homebrewing* (1991), edited the first and second editions of the book. He writes that *Brewing Lager Beer* "has become a standard for aspiring and veteran small brewers everywhere. Greg's devotees sometimes refer to themselves as 'Noonanites.'"

The wiry son of teetotaler Irish-American parents, Noonan was known for going out of his way to help fellow brewers with technical issues or to track down supplies. He and Egelston, who had known each other as homebrewers who bought their supplies at Northampton's Beer and Wine Hobby, pooled their malt shipments to save money. Noonan helped a fellow homebrewer, John Korpita, launch the Amherst Brewing Company in Massachusetts, even designing the brewpub's logo.

He also mentored the younger brewers who worked for him, encouraging their passion and drilling proper technique into their heads. "He could be a tough taskmaster," says Noonan's brother Jerome, but his protégés "all learned a lot from that." He adds that, after Greg passed away in 2010, he "was flabbergasted when they talked about how big a factor he was in their lives." Some of those Noonanites are rather accomplished. They include John Kimmich of Waterbury, Vermont's Alchemist Brewery, whose Heady Topper IPA has been ranked the number-one beer in the world by both Beer Advocate and Rate Beer; Shaun Hill of Hill Farmstead in Greensboro, Vermont, who brews several unique beers that are considered world-class; and Glenn Walter of Three Needs taproom in Burlington, who—under Greg's tutelage—created the popular style of beer known as black IPA.

In its early years, the Vermont Pub & Brewery experienced a phenomenon familiar to other craft breweries across the country at that time. On the one hand, people flocked to experience this exotic new place that actually *made* the beer it served. On the other hand, they didn't fully grasp the notion. While "some people were thrilled" by the beer offerings, says Nancy Noonan, "others would order Bud and, when they couldn't get it, they'd walk away. 'What do you mean you make your own beer?' It was an outlandish concept."

Nobody knew what craft beer was, remembers Peter Egelston. "Frankly, most people didn't care what it was. Beer was beer. Beer was a commodity." He remembers a waiter on the Northampton Brewery's opening day telling a customer about the two beers on tap, a golden lager and an amber lager. ("That was all we thought we'd ever need," Egelston chuckles.) "The fellow at the table said, 'Yeah, just give me an American beer.'" The waiter asked which of the two house-brewed beers he would prefer. Still not getting it, the customer again ordered an "American beer." That's when the waiter threw up his hands and said, "'Buddy, the beer is made right there through the glass about 15 feet from where you're sitting. It doesn't get any more American than that,'" laughs Egelston.

He and his fellow publicans found their footing soon enough as excitement about local beer spread. Their establishments survived and thrived. Within a few years of starting the Northampton Brewery, Peter and Janet Egelston would open the Portsmouth Brewery, New Hampshire's first brewpub, and Peter would buy the briefly revived Frank Jones brewery and turn it into Smuttynose, the Granite State's first successful microbrewery. The Noonans, despite divorcing in 1992, opened another brewpub, the Seven Barrel Brewery, in Lebanon, New Hampshire, in 1994.

Several other notable brewpubs cropped up in the late 1980s and early 1990s: Gritty McDuff's in Portland (which later expanded to locations in Freeport and Auburn), famous for its Black Fly Stout; Boston Beer Works near Fenway Park (later with additional pubs near Boston North Station, Salem, and Lowell); McNeill's Brewery, a stripped-down tavern with a wonderfully weird vibe in Brattleboro, Vermont; John Harvard's Brewhouse, which started in Harvard Square and has five other locations throughout the

Ed Stebbins and Richard Pfeffer, founders of Gritty McDuff's brewpubs, courtesy of Gritty McDuffs.

Northeast, including Union Station in Providence; and the City Steam Brewery Café in Hartford, Connecticut's Brown Thomson & Company building, an architectural landmark.

Ed Stebbins, who has co-owned Gritty McDuff's with Richard Pfeffer since 1988, remembers the sense of optimism during this period. "We were convinced that we were going to go into packaging, and we were going to be bottling, and we would have our beer in fifty states within ten years," he says with a smile. It seemed entirely plausible.

———◆———

While New England brewpubs were busy educating drinkers about what an American beer could be, their fellow breweries on the production side were striving to get their beverages into consumers' hands via six-pack or bar tap. Like Geary's, they were turned down by banks and had to seek funding from family and friends. They mostly distributed their own product at first, because wholesalers ignored them. They played up their beers' intense flavor and sense of place, contrasting them with those bland megabrews from nowhere. Their marketing strategy was often as simple as a guy showing up at prospective accounts and saying, "Hey, try this great new local beer. We bottled it last night."

Some of those fledgling enterprises evolved into regional breweries, the modern-day counterparts to Industrial Era notables such as Narragansett, Hull, Frank Jones, and Harvard. We're talking Harpoon, Shipyard, Magic Hat, and Long Trail—the four largest breweries born and based in New England. Most of their beer is sold in the Northeast, but it is also available in many other states. Though none of the above are as big as the king of New England breweries, 'Gansett, was in its heyday, they are among the top

Harpoon owners Rich Doyle and Dan Kenary during the brewery's early years, courtesy of Harpoon Brewery.

twenty largest craft breweries in the United States. Their varying paths to success provide a snapshot of the evolution of craft brewing in the 1990s and 2000s, with its wild growth, push-and-pull with Big Beer, and mergers and acquisitions.

The Harpoon Brewery, originally called the Massachusetts Bay Brewing Company, started in 1987 in a warehouse on the South Boston waterfront. Harvard classmates Rich Doyle and Dan Kenary, who traveled in Europe and loved the beer culture they found there, built the first production brewery in Massachusetts since Prohibition, returning local brewing to a city that once boasted thirty beer producers. As their business grew, it played a part in the neighborhood's transformation from a gritty wasteland to the convention and destination-dining mecca it is today.

With a third partner, George Ligetti, Doyle and Kenary raised $430,000 from family, friends, and acquaintances, installed some JV Northwest equipment in their building on Northern Avenue, and hired twenty-three-year-old Russ Heissner to brew their flagship Harpoon Ale, a malty, slightly fruity American amber. Many early craft breweries nurtured their clienteles on this approachable style of beer.

Growth was decent those first few years, but far from robust. The future of the brewery was shaky enough that, when Harpoon held its first Octoberfest in 1990, it was considered "a bit of a hail mary pass," according to the company history. "[The partners] had always wanted to host a festival at the brewery as an ode to the great Munich fall festival, so they thought this might be one last hurrah." Luckily, two thousand people turned up to sing "Ein Prosit," and a company tradition was born. Then, in 1993, came another boost. Tod Mott—who'd turned to brewing after earning an MFA in ceramics—created a new seasonal beer: Harpoon IPA. He came to Harpoon after an internship at Vermont's Catamount Brewing Company and had been with Harpoon a mere two years.

At that time, there were very few beers in the country outside of the Pacific Northwest showcasing the distinctive hops of that region.

Mott married those hops with a traditional English style, an India pale ale. To further distinguish the beer, he incorporated toasted malt—which Harpoon employees toasted in their own ovens at home—and dry-hopping. Mott explains, "To dry hop the beer, we stuffed two pairs of pantyhose with five pounds of [Cascade hops] in each pair and placed the 'legs' into the conditioning tank. The IPA sat on the dry hops for about ten days as the beer conditioned."

This practice, which imparts the citrus/floral/herbal/pine characteristics of hops to a beer rather than the bitterness that comes from adding hops earlier in the brewing process, is common in today's world of hop-heavy styles. But hardly anyone was doing it twenty years ago. "It was a VERY extreme beer for 1993," Harpoon declares. It was one of the highlights of the Boston Brewers Festival that year. The late British beer writer Michael Jackson, who was signing books at the event, fondly pronounced it "very hoppy." Much to Doyle's and Kenary's surprise, Harpoon IPA was a hit. "It quickly became our bestselling beer and transformed the company. Our IPA made Harpoon the brewery it is today." That's saying something—Harpoon is the largest independent brewery in New England and eighth-largest craft brewery in the country. Its two plants, the original one in Boston, which now boasts a spacious beer hall overlooking a brand-new cannery, and one in Windsor, Vermont, produce two hundred thousand barrels of beer annually.

The year he created its IPA, Mott left Harpoon and worked at the Commonwealth Brewing Company and then the Back Bay Brewing Company, which was a gastropub before there were gastropubs. Think of Mott as the anti-Jim Koch—meaning that on the Rich and Famous Spectrum, Mott would represent one end of distinguished New England brewers, and Koch would represent the other. Mott is not nearly as well known or financially successful as Koch, but he is highly respected among industry peers. The first brewery he owned, Quincy Ships in the Budweiser stronghold of Quincy, Massachusetts, lasted only a year. Mostly, he's been a journeyman, taking his recipes from brewhouse to brewhouse, making delicious beer and training assistants to do the same. Although he's proud of having created Harpoon IPA, not to mention the Portsmouth Brewery's famous Kate the Great Imperial Stout, he doesn't beat his chest about it. His career, for better or worse, has been a very Yankee one. Mott most recently embarked on a new venture, Tributary Brewing, in an old Red & White grocery store in Kittery, Maine.

Harpoon's closest competitors in terms of production are Shipyard in Portland, Maine, and Magic Hat in Burlington, Vermont, which each put out more than one hundred and fifty thousand barrels annually. Both started in 1994 as producers of ale fermented with Ringwood yeast—that "controversial" strain with which British biochemist and brewing consultant Alan Pugsley, formulator of Geary's Pale Ale, launched copious New England craft breweries. Similarities between the two breweries end there.

Shipyard, the first brewery Pugsley called his own, paid tribute to Portland's maritime heritage. Its flagship (a term that could not be more appropriate here) was Shipyard Export, a Yankee homage to Canada's Molson Export that Pugsley first produced at Kennebunkport Brewing, his partner Fred Forsley's brewpub a few miles down the coast. Pugsley's reputation was such that, when the Miller Brewing Company went looking for craft producers to add to its portfolio in 1995, it made Shipyard an enticing offer: We'll buy a 50 percent stake in your company, and you can expand and make more beer so that we can market and distribute it nationwide. Woo hoo!

Those were boom times. Anheuser-Busch purchased a 25 percent stake in Washington's Redhook Brewery, a deal that included the construction of a brand new facility in Portsmouth, New Hampshire. Some New England brewers felt threatened by this, including Jim Koch, who denounced the partnership as "Budhook." In 1995, Redhook was the first craft brewery to go public. Boston Beer Company was right on its heels.

Shipyard expanded under the deal with Miller, but the marketing and distribution side of things fizzled. The big brewery became distracted by its lite-beer war with Anheuser-Busch. Sales of Shipyard slid. Pugsley and Forsley forged ahead, used their extra capacity to contract brew, and eventually bought back Miller's interest in the company in 2000. The fact that production has gone up every year since vindicates the partners' decision to split with their aloof benefactor.

In recent years, the brewery's stalwart maritime identity has fallen by the wayside as Shipyard Pumpkinhead and Seadog Wild Blueberry ales have become its top sellers. When he goes out for a pop, Pugsley prefers a Shipyard Export (number three in the portfolio), or perhaps a Geary's or a Sierra Nevada. Speaking admiringly of the latter brewery's founder and owner, Ken Grossman, the Englishman says, "He's never gone queer with fruits and things." Pugsley recently sold his stake in Shipyard to Forsley in order to start his own consultancy, through which he remains connected to the company.

Two hundred miles northeast in Burlington, Magic Hat emerged in 1994 as New England's hippie brewery. Alan Newman, who co-founded the eco-conscious cleaning-product company Seventh Generation, and his partner, brewer Bob Johnson, put trippy-looking labels on beers such as Number 9, an apricot-tinged ale, and Hocus Pocus, a pale wheat ale. With the Vermont Pub & Brewery having laid the groundwork, Magic Hat—whose full name is actually Magic Hat Brewery and Performing Arts Center—cemented Burlington as a destination for craft beer, not only through its products but through a huge annual Mardi Gras party. It was so successful by 2006 that Newman sold a majority interest in the company to a Connecticut hedge fund, Basso Capital Management, in order to acquire one of the biggest names in West Coast craft brewing, the Pyramid Brewery of Seattle.

Then things got weird. After the Great Recession hit in 2008, Basso, against Newman's wishes, sold Magic Hat/Pyramid to North

Alan Pugsley, courtesy of Shipyard Brewing Company.

American Breweries, makers of Labatt Blue and Genesee, among other brands. That's when Newman bailed. Then, in 2012, NAB was acquired by Florida Farm & Ice, a beverage company in Costa Rica. So, while Magic Hat is still brewed in Vermont, it's no longer an American company. Who could have predicted that outcome in 1994? As for Newman, who sports a thick, grey beard and canary-yellow spectacles, he came out of semi-retirement recently to lend his entrepreneurial creativity to Boston Beer Company's start-up incubator, Alchemy & Science.

While Shipyard and Magic Hat were just getting started, Long Trail was building a bigger house. The brewery that former electrical engineer Andy Pherson started in 1989 in an old woolen mill in central Vermont had by 1994 outgrown its original space. The packaging of its German altbier-inspired Long Trail Ale—a member of the accessible amber family—represented the flipside of Magic Hat's hippie: the outdoorsy hiker/skier. Pherson built a new brewery on a picturesque nook of the Ottauqueechee River and amped up production of its beers—including a popular strong ale called Double Bag. And did so while setting a gold standard of environmental stewardship through tight water conservation and heat recovery, among others.

In 2006, Pherson sold his company and has lately turned to a new trade: gold prospecting. Seriously. He pans for gold on the same river where he built his brewery, the Ottauqueechee, as well as in Colorado. Long Trail's new owner, the private equity firm Fulham & Company, purchased Otter Creek/Wolaver's Organic Ales of Middlebury and The Shed of Stowe, creating the fourth-largest craft brewery in New England. It collectively produces one hundred and forty thousand barrels of beer annually. Long Trail Ale has the distinction of being the top selling beer in a state that has the most breweries per capita in the nation.

The volume of beer you brew isn't everything, of course. New England boasts several smaller but well-established micros that came of age in the 1990s, including the Allagash Brewing Company in Maine; the Berkshire Brewing Company, Ipswich Ale Brewery, and Wachusett Brewing Company in Massachusetts; the Smuttynose Brewing Company and Tuckerman's Brewing Company in New Hampshire; and Cisco Brewers on Nantucket Island, which also boasts a winery and a distillery.

———◆———

The 1990s craft beer industry was full of contradictions. Its growth was robust and fragile. Beer drinkers were excited about microbrews and indifferent to them. Craft beer seemed to be everywhere, yet it made up only about 3 percent of the U.S. market. Meanwhile, megabrewers tried to hone in on the market—jockeying between hindering the craft beer movement and helping it to grow,

Smuttynose's lead brewer Dan Schubert, courtesy of Robert Lussier.

depending on what was best for their bottom line, of course. And Jim Koch, who would emerge from the 1990s as the king of craft brewers, was a hated and admired figure among his brethren.

Remember how it took ten years for the Anchor Brewery just to turn a profit? Well, by 1995, times had changed. A decade after the Boston Beer Company sold its first case of Sam Adams, it became a publicly traded company. That milestone signified how fast craft beer was growing upon the foundation laid by Fritz Maytag, as well as the strength of Koch's contract-based business model and entrepreneurial drive. In the mid-1990s, Boston Beer was successfully competing with not only imports but also another big contract brewer, Pete's Wicked Ale of California. (Remember Pete's Wicked Ale?) Since contract brewers rent the space and personnel of existing breweries instead of building their own, they can focus profits on sales and marketing instead of tanks and plumbing and sell more beer. Koch was not the first to make beer this way, and the practice is more widespread today than ever. But the slender, reedy-voiced mogul has been the most successful contract brewer ever.

That success bred opposition from smaller craft brewers on the one hand and Big Beer on the other. New England brewers who spent tons of money and sweat building their facilities from scratch called bullshit on the Sam Adams brand's association with Boston and New England history, as well as its claims of being hand-crafted. Koch and his beer recipe came from German ancestry in the Midwest, and 99 percent of his product was manufactured outside Massachusetts at big breweries like Stroh's. Plus, the beer's namesake wasn't even a brewer! (If you recall, Samuel Adams made malt, unsuccessfully, before his political career took off.)

Then there was the fact that Koch made unsavory moves, like suing the Boston Beer Works brewpub over using "Boston Beer" in its name. The Beer Works won the suit but had to spend a lot of time and money doing so. Koch, who favored suits and a clean shave over Carhartts and a beard, got under the skin of those for whom "local" and "handmade" were almost sacred concepts. Brewers were supposed to be passionate artisans trading advice, not cutthroat competitors suing each other.

But if smaller craft brewers thought Boston Beer's business practices were threatening, they had only to consider "100 percent share of mind." That was what Anheuser-Busch called its mid-1990s initiative to essentially strong-arm distributors into focusing on A-B brands at the expense of microbrews. Craft beer constituted a mere wavelet in the ocean that A-B dominated, but the megabrewer saw the segment's double-digit growth and did its best to nip it in the bud—when it wasn't getting a piece of action, that is, as in the case of Redhook.

A-B also lobbied for "truth in labeling," aiming right at contract brewers like Boston Beer and Pete's. In an infamous 1996 *Dateline* exposé on contract brewers, and in its own advertising, A-B called out Jim Koch for putting the Boston address of his company headquarters on each label of Sam Adams, rather than the brewery where the product was actually made. Never mind that A-B was producing "phantom craft" beers like Red Wolf and Pacific Ridge Pale Ale to compete with microbrews like Sierra Nevada. These beers also competed with other phantoms, such as Miller's Red Dog and Coors' Killians Red and Blue Moon. Koch countered A-B's labeling campaign with one of his own, calling for brewers to put a best-before date on their packaging. He was the only craft brewer with enough clout to engage in such a fight.

Craft brewers eventually realized that Koch was more an advocate for their industry than an antagonist. David Geary had tuned into this idea early on. When six-packs of Sam Adams started appearing at Rite-Aid stores in Maine next to Geary's Pale Ale, he didn't panic; he was relieved. "Now we have a category," he said. And when Sam Adams-bashing was in full swing during a Brewers Association conference in Boston in 1996, he scolded attendees for questioning whether Koch was a craft brewer. "He taught us all how to sell craft beer," Geary reminded them in his curmudgeonly but incisive way.

Another reason craft brewers learned to stop worrying and love Sam was that "made in Pennsylvania" vs. "made in New England" was a non-issue for the vast majority of craft beer drinkers, who cared more about whether the liquid in the bottle tasted good and was priced fairly. Pherson of Long Trail recalls, "We were all beating the drums against Samuel Adams, because the beer wasn't made in Boston. Then we all stopped, because we found that the consumers didn't really care. And when we found that the consumers didn't care whether the beer was imported, we went from 'Product of the

United States' to 'Brewed in Vermont.'"

All of craft beer's internal bickering over contract, vs. local, publicly traded vs. mom-and-pop, together with the uncertainty Big Beer sowed about the definition of "craft," tarnished the image of microbrews in New England and around the country. But the shakeout that occurred in the late 1990s and early 2000s had much less to do with "Budhook" vs. Sam Adams vs. Long Trail than with mismanagement and irrational exuberance.

"I generally hated the groups of lawyers who got together and hired a homebrewer to build some brewery," said Ray McNeill, equally famous for his eponymous brewpub in Brattleboro, Vermont, and his blustery persona. "A lot of those people went out of business, thankfully, because they had no business being in the industry."

Between 1996 and 2000, roughly two hundred breweries closed around the country, and craft beer's annual growth percentages slid to single-digits. In *The Audacity of Hops*, Acitelli sums up the crash this way: "There was too much beer, a lot of it of dubious quality, and too many breweries, brewpubs, and contract brewers, the latter dominated by entities that might not have been in the movement for the craftsmanship."

———◆———

Unfortunately, a few who *were* in the movement for the craftsmanship became casualties of the shakeout. That's the story of Catamount, the second microbrewery to open in New England. Named after the mountain lion believed to have become extinct in the region in the late 1800s, Catamount started the same year as Geary's, 1986, but didn't deliver its first cases until early 1987. It primarily brewed Catamount Amber, a classic British pale ale, and Catamount Gold, a hoppy-for-its-day blonde ale. Head brewer Steve Mason apprenticed at a small brewery in England in 1983 after having homebrewed since college in the 1970s.

Mason briefly taught physical education before embarking on his brewing adventure in a turn-of-the-century meat warehouse on the Vermont-New Hampshire border. His business partners were Alan Davis, a bluegrass musician, and Steve Israel, an organic beef farmer and salvage-business owner who made art and architecture out of reclaimed objects. As far as case studies go, you couldn't invent a better team of eccentrics.

Mason was a meticulous brewer. His beers were high quality and consistent—a rare achievement among small brewers in those days. Catamount Gold won a gold medal at the Great American Beer Festival in 1989. Like the Commonwealth Brewing Company in Boston and Greg Noonan of the Vermont Pub & Brewery, Mason trained a raft of apprentices who went on to notable careers, including Tod Mott, Paul Sayler of Zero Gravity Brewing in Burlington, Vermont, and Tony Lubold of New Hampshire's Seven Barrel Brewery.

"[Mason] was one of the most important people in my brewing career," says Sayler, who started apprenticing for Mason in 1990 and stayed for five years. "Steve taught me to be a technical brewer. Catamount ran impressive batteries of tests; the lab was always busy."

For the first few years, Catamount beers pretty much sold themselves. Davis said in an *Inc.* magazine interview that sales-and-marketing operations consisted of "me in a car going around to accounts." Like Jim Koch a couple of years before, the partners knew that if they could just get their product in front of retailers, they'd be on their way.

While Catamount's production grew, it also—what? yes—contract-brewed for several companies, including Frank Jones, Commonwealth Brewing, Post Road, McNeill's, and the Brooklyn Brewery.

In the mid-1990s, the brewery began constructing a brand-new three-million-dollar facility in Windsor, Vermont. Mason and the brewery's board of directors figured that high-quality beer would continue to sell itself, and in greater volume than before. Davis says he advocated early on for a greater emphasis on promotional efforts, such as hiring more salespeople and providing Catamount swag to retailers, but he was overruled. He left the company in 1993.

By the time the Windsor brewery opened in 1997, the craft beer market had flattened out, and there were many more brands competing for the slice of the pie that remained. Catamount had a lot of beer to sell, and it wasn't moving. Meanwhile, there was this gleaming new facility to pay for. The company ended up crushed by debt. "With a lot of companies, [they] try to expand a little too quickly," says Israel. "When you're pioneering something, there's a huge learning curve." The Windsor brewery went to auction in 2000, and Harpoon made the very sound investment of one million dollars to nab the place. Catamount's pain was Harpoon's gain. That's how shakeouts work.

Mason has since left the world of beer making. As much as David Geary, Alan Pugsley, Greg Noonan, or Peter and Janet Egelston, he helped invent modern New England brewing. He may have made some faulty business decisions, but then so did a lot of craft brewers who managed to survive the crash. In a way, he was just unlucky.

Sayler says, "When you look at how many of those places that opened on a wing and prayer survived, it's amazing." It really is.

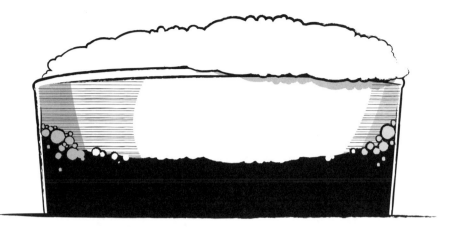

ℛefermentation

At the Allagash Brewery in Portland, Maine, there is a 70° F cellar where thousands of brown bottles sit quietly as the beer inside them referments. *Does that mean it turns into whiskey or something?* No. It means that before it's bottled, the beer is mixed with a tiny bit of sugar and fresh yeast. The yeast devour the sugar, and—voilà, the beer is naturally carbonated in the bottle.

This refermentation, also known as bottle conditioning, is one of the signatures of the Belgian-style beers that Allagash makes. When done right, bottle conditioning creates bubbles that are fine and dense, rather than fizzy like a soda, and that form a fluffy head. It also allows the myriad of flavors produced by the mingling of malt, hops, and yeast to further evolve. (Winemakers, by the way, got the idea for champagne from brewers and their bottle-conditioned beers.)

Another way for beer to referment is with a cask. Common in the

United Kingdom, cask-conditioned ale, also called real ale, is put into a keg unfiltered near the end of its primary fermentation. As the yeast complete their mission in the new vessel, a small amount of carbonation develops while the beer "drops bright," a.k.a. while its sediment floats to the bottom of the cask.

NERAX, which sounds like a Cold War missile program but is actually the longest-running real ale festival in the United States—the New England Real Ale Exhibition—is a good place to see and taste cask ale. Stacked on their sides, casks from breweries in Great Britain and New England take in air, rather than carbon dioxide, as the ale is pumped through long-handled taps called beer engines. Air will eventually spoil beer, but there's a magical window of time in which it brings out fine aromas and flavors. It's like letting wine breathe. Over the course of its lifespan, which ideally shouldn't last longer than a few days, cask ale evolves, living second, even third lives.

Craft beer, which reintroduced the wonders of traditional brewing methods to the American palate, is itself enjoying a new life. It has evolved to a point no one could have predicted after the crash of the late 1990s. Several years ago it entered a phase of growth that still has beer enthusiasts pinching themselves. As of 2014, there were 3,464 breweries in the United States, 3,418 of which were craft breweries. That's the highest total since the pre-Prohibition golden era of the 1880s. In fact, we've never had as many breweries as we do now. In New England, there are well over two hundred breweries, the vast majority of them small.

If you want a real-life example of craft beer's evolution in New England, consider Allagash. Rob Tod, who grew up near Concord, Massachusetts, started the brewery in 1994. He had worked construction jobs after college and then decided to go to graduate school for geology. He envisioned becoming a professor. Living in Vermont and seeking employment while applying to schools, he followed a tip from a friend who said that the Otter Creek Brewery in Middlebury was looking for a keg washer.

"I walked into the brewery and was like, 'Wow, this is cool,'" recalls Tod. "I like working with my hands—I love plumbing, welding, carpentry, pumps, motors, tanks. There's a lot of art involved in [brewing], and there's also a lot of science. I just liked all three of those aspects: the mechanical end, the art, the science. In forty-eight hours, I was hooked." Alarming his parents, he canceled his plans for graduate school. He worked at Otter Creek for a year and then moved to Portland to start Allagash, named for a river in northern Maine. He wrote much of his business plan sipping Black Fly Stout at Gritty McDuff's. "I was very naïve," he says, "about what it would take to start a brewery." Especially a Belgian brewery.

If people were still iffy on the merits of English- and West Coast-style ambers, pales, and porters at that point, imagine how they felt about Belgian beer. We're not talking about anything as pedestrian as Stella Artois, a standard continental lager that happens to come from Belgium. We're talking older, odder styles that arose from Belgium being a crossroad of the world's great beer and wine regions: witbier, dubbel, tripel, lambic, gueuze. Tod was

Rob Tod (left) in the early days of Allagash, courtesy of Allagash Brewery.

inspired by the "almost limitless potential of the Belgian brewing tradition." He chose the witbier, or white beer, style as his flagship. It is an ale made with both malted and unmalted wheat and fermented with a type of yeast that brewers call "expressive." It is subtly dosed with coriander and curaçao orange peel. Because of the unmalted, or "raw" wheat, the beer is so cloudy it's almost opaque. It smells wonderful—tangy, bready, and spicy—but it doesn't smell like most people's concept of beer.

"I used to walk into accounts, pour samples, and the first thing they'd say is, 'What's wrong with it? Why does it look weird?,'" says Tod, who wears button-down shirts and wire-rimmed glasses and could easily pass for that geology professor he once aspired to be. He brewed a mere 120 barrels his first year. The average brewpub at that time was producing ten times that. Over the first decade, production slowly rose to three thousand barrels. "Just to stay in business, we ended up in twenty-nine states," says Tod. It was a dozen years before appreciation for Belgian beer hit a critical mass.

"As the craft beer business has evolved, people have gotten more curious about what's out there in terms of flavor and aroma experiences. The white has become a style that's pretty commonplace now. You can go into restaurants in Boston or Los Angeles or Chicago and buy an Allagash White." The brewery makes dozens of styles now, including Allagash Black, a Belgian-style stout, and Curieux, a strong, golden "tripel" ale aged in bourbon barrels. And instead of fanning out nationwide, Allagash now distributes to only three key regions—the Northeast, California, and the Chicago area—where demand is greatest.

"In the last seven or eight years, we've gone from three thousand to sixty thousand barrels." Tod doesn't pump his fist in the air, or even pause for effect, after uttering this remarkable statistic. He's like one of those movie stars who becomes famous after years of obscurity and gladly skips the red-carpet preening to focus on meaty new roles. For Tod, those "roles" are experiments like his

Coolship series of spontaneously fermented, lambic-style beers and anything that arises from his barrel-aging room, which is a sight (and smell) to behold. Tod is happy to share what he has learned on his slog toward success. He has been a willing mentor to notable startups such as the Maine Beer Company and Rising Tide Brewing Company. And he gets invitations to speak at events like the Innovators@Google series of talks. His parents, by the way, came around to their son's career choice. "They're happy with the way things are going now," Tod says.

———◆———

It's not just Belgian-style beer that people are clamoring for—it's anything unusual or extreme. If you've visited a beer bar lately, you've probably noticed that the menu seems to consist of a dozen IPAs and imperial stouts trying to outdo each other in hoppiness and alcohol content. But Extreme-Beer Mania is just the most in-your-face aspect of craft beer's new wave. There are, in reality, dozens of styles to suit just about anyone's palate. You can walk into many fine restaurants in Boston, Providence, or Portland and order an artisanal farmhouse ale or well-crafted lager. You can drive all over Vermont and Maine for weeks and never get the same local beer twice at any pub or store. In New Hampshire, the number of breweries has surged to twenty-three (and counting), thanks to recent legislation encouraging tiny startups called nanobreweries. Yankee beer drinkers are so spoiled!

There are many reasons for this surge in quality breweries. The most basic one is that brewers never stopped making good beer. Many of them weathered the shakeout, and, though craft beer was no longer The Coolest New Thing, they kept doing the thing they loved: experimenting with new styles and making better and better beer. They made liberal use of new hop varieties that have proliferated out of the Pacific Northwest, New Zealand, and Japan, among other regions.

In addition to learning on the job, they also educated themselves at programs such as the American Brewers Guild in Salisbury, Vermont.

Meanwhile, a whole new generation came along that grew up with microbrews. When they turned twenty-one, they could go into a store and choose not just between Coors, PBR, and Heineken, but between several dozen brands and styles of beer from megabreweries, microbreweries, and everything in between. They became fluent in craft beer at a young age and had higher expectations for quality and variety than earlier generations did.

Restaurant and bar owners also became fluent in craft beer. Beer enthusiasts used to bitch to whomever would listen that, while any decent restaurant had a heavy binder listing the wines in the house, its beer selection comprised a same-old, same-old collection of megabrews, big imports, and, if you were lucky, Sam Adams, Sierra Nevada, and perhaps one local brew whose presence in the region was too prominent for even indifferent bar managers to ignore. 'Look, here's our hometown beer! Oh, it's not a style you like? How about a Blue Moon, then?' Gradually, bar managers heard all the

Courtesy of Deep Ellum.

pleas for a better beer selection. At the cutting edge of this development is a new figure in the culinary world: the cicerone, beer's equivalent of the sommelier.

Craft beer used to exist in a sort of extra-culinary enclave. You could only find it at brewpubs and bars where it was the main attraction; food was kind of an afterthought. If you weren't in the mood for wings, burgers, or British pub fare, you were out of luck. Now, good beer is part of the culinary landscape. Locavores and foodies demand quality malt beverages to wash down their pork-belly tacos and heirloom turnips—which means that more and more women, who make up at least half of these groups, are drinking craft beer. Craft-beer enthusiasts used to cluster together like first-generation immigrants. Now they're more widely distributed and more diverse.

Not that beer geeks don't have plenty of venues in which to associate with their own kind. Beer bars have proliferated to fill this role and help kick-start a new wave of excitement about craft beer. At a beer bar, you can sample microbrews from all the over the country, as well as off-the-beaten-path imports. New England's pioneer in this sector is the Great Lost Bear, a beloved Portland, Maine, institution that opened in 1979 and started serving microbrews the minute Geary's opened in 1986. They specialize in beers from the Northeast, especially Maine, and have sixty-nine taps.

Beginning in the early 2000s, the beer bar concept started to get traction. Many of the new bars were owned or run by young staffers who could speak knowledgably about beer while their iPods provided funky background music. At places like the Publick House, Lord Hobo, Deep Ellum, Armsby Abby, and Dirty Truth in Massachusetts; Ebenezer's and Novare Res in Maine; Prohibition Pig and Three Penny Taproom in Vermont; Track 84 and Wild Colonial in Rhode Island; and Cask Republic and Willimantic Brewing Company (which is also a brewpub) in Connecticut, part of the experience is bantering with the staff and other customers about a particular beer's maker or ingredients—or just reading a book and quietly enjoying the scene. These bars are where the beer geek and the hipster meld.

———◇———

The early twenty-first century evolution of craft beer is closely intertwined with another evolution—that of the digital world. When the first big wave of craft breweries emerged in the 1990s, the World Wide Web was in its infancy, most people connected to the Internet via AOL, and online communities lived in "chat rooms." Engaging with customers online was pretty much limited to a brewer emailing a recipe for Scotch ale to a dedicated fan. Then came BeerAdvocate.com.

Massachusetts brothers Todd and Jason Alström started a website in 1996 as a way to compile and publish their own reviews of beers. Their interest in the sudsy stuff began when Todd was stationed

Todd and Jason Alström of BeerAdvocate.com,
courtesy of Todd Alström.

in England while in the U.S. Air Force during the late 1980s and early 1990s. Jason visited his older brother, and the two went pub-hopping, discovering the wonders of Old World beers. Back in the United States, they visited craft breweries and sampled everything, posting online what they saw, smelled, and tasted in a beer. In 2000, they named their site BeerAdvocate.com and opened it up to other users, urging them to "Respect Beer." Fellow enthusiasts could log in and rate a particular brew, as well as engage with other members of the community in forums. Todd's training as a programmer enabled the brothers to maintain a user-friendly, flexible platform that could handle escalating traffic. And escalate it did.

BeerAdvocate has 2.5 million monthly visitors and contains hundreds of thousands of beers and millions of reviews. In 2006, the Alströms launched a print magazine, *Beer Advocate*, whose readership is estimated at 150,000. Their regular beer events in Boston, including the Extreme Beer and American Craft Beer Fests, attract thousands of attendees.

Aside from pure beer geekery, the community is knit together by the Alströms' promise not to sell out to commercial interests and by the rules of conduct enforced by the brothers' constant presence on the site. They're like a couple of even-tempered chaperones breaking up the hissy fits that often show up in forum discussions.

Brewers both appreciate and denounce the influence of BeerAdvocate.com and competing sites such as RateBeer.com. On the one hand, these sites spread knowledge around and get consumers passionate about beer. On the other hand, their collective taste can be narrow. BeerAdvocate's Top 250 list is heavily dominated by beers that are high in alcohol, hops, or both. It's not that these aren't great beers, but there are great beers out there whose flavors are more subtle. Massachusetts brewer Chris Lohring, who makes "session" beers (low-alcohol beers that can be drunk in quantity) under his Notch label, realized early on that he had to abandon "any desire to try to win people over who don't get it."

In 2005, the Alström brothers decided that the New England beer scene needed some love. They held their first-ever festival dedicated to beer from the region in October that year. In promoting the event, Todd said, "There are so many beers available these days that it's easy to forget what's in your own backyard. New England Beer Fest is a reminder to look, and our nod to the region's brewers and its rich brewing history."

That New Englanders needed to be reminded to drink local beer gives you an idea of what our brewing scene was like during those early years of the twenty-first century. It's not that the breweries that opened in the 1990s and survived the shakeout weren't rolling along, and even growing. It's that they were doing so slowly and/or quietly. To be sure, many of those businesses were brewpubs serving a very local market.

Few breweries opened in New England between 2000 and 2008. Meanwhile, at Boston-area beer bars, the taps were flowing with hoppy beers from a relatively new crop of West Coast breweries like Stone and Lagunitas, and from boutique European outfits like De Ranke in Belgium. The New England beer scene seemed to be suffering from a lack of both new blood and native support.

Perhaps because of our history as both a shipping capital and a region less-than-ideally suited to farming, New Englanders have eagerly embraced beverages from elsewhere. *Porter from London? Lager from St. Louis? IPA from Oregon? Keep it coming.* Yet, in addition to sharing in the nationwide revival of interest in local, small-batch food and drink, New Englanders have pride in their own tradition of Yankee craftsmanship: making quality goods with the resources at hand and selling them to your neighbor. As the second decade of the twenty-first century dawned, brewers woke up and said something like, "It's about time New England had a damn fine new beer, and I'm going to brew it." When they carried out their plans, they were pleasantly surprised by the reception they got.

Dann Paquette, a veteran New England brewer, started Pretty Things Beer and Ale Project with his wife, Martha Simpson-Holley, in 2008. The couple's life savings of eight thousand dollars served as the company's sole investment. The truth was, Dann couldn't find a job. At that time in New England, there wasn't much use "for brewers like me who want to come in and be the head creative guy."

He had bounced around ever since his first attempt at starting a brand—a Belgian-style golden ale called Rapscallion—fizzled. Previously, he had made a name for himself in the 1990s as someone who went out on a stylistic limb working at the North East Brewing Company, a brewpub in the Allston neighborhood of Boston. (A casualty of the shakeout, North East closed in 2002.) While working at The Tap, a brewpub in Haverhill, Massachusetts, he met his future wife and business partner at, appropriately enough, NERAX.

Dann Paquette and Martha Simpson-Holley of Pretty Things Beer and Ale Project, courtesy of Martha Simpson-Holley.

Their marriage led Dann to a two-year stint working at the Daleside Brewery in Martha's native Yorkshire, England, where he absorbed British brewing techniques and beer culture. When the couple returned to the States, Martha, a microbiologist, landed a job in a research laboratory at MIT, while Dann launched their "project" at the Paper City Brewing Company in Holyoke, Massachusetts. He brewed his own beer using Paper City's equipment. This tenant-brewer arrangement has turned out to be a popular strategy in craft brewing's second wave.

Inspired by fellow brewer Phil Markowski's book, *Farmhouse Ales: Culture and Craftsmanship in the Belgian Tradition* (2004), Dann had a clear idea of what his flagship would be: a "hoppy, golden and dry" Belgian saison called Jack D'Or. His creation tasted like it had been brewed for a hundred years, and yet it was fresh and new. It also paired well with food and looked elegant in its custom stemmed glass. Dann and Martha spent all their money producing that initial sixteen-barrel batch and getting it out to the market. If it made a profit, then they'd be able to make a second batch, and so on. Luckily, Jack D'Or was an instant hit. "The Boston that we came back to was really different," says Dann. "There became a real local demand for beer."

Today, Dann and Martha produce four thousand barrels of beer annually at the Buzzards Bay Brewing Company in Westport, Massachusetts. Like Jack D'Or, all of Pretty Things' quirkily branded beers—e.g. St. Botolph's Town, a Yorkshire brown ale, and Fluffy White Rabbits, a Belgian tripel—have a sort of Old World-meets-New World quality, combining aspects of Belgian, British, and American craft brewing. They have proliferated among good restaurants and bars in Massachusetts, inspiring other boutique beers. *Oprah Magazine* named Jack D'Or one of the nation's ten best U.S. microbrews. Nevertheless, Dann and Martha intend to keep Pretty Things small and local. They run everything themselves—including producing the artwork for their labels—and they like it that way.

Within the last few years, Vermont added to its distinction of having the most breweries per capita by also having the most rock-star brewers per capita. If you're a beer geek, you already know that I'm talking about John Kimmich, Shaun Hill, and Sean Lawson. Actually, "rock star" inaptly describes these guys. They're more like eighteenth-century classical composers, whose fame was widespread but if you wanted to hear their music you had to travel to Vienna. BeerAdvocate.com ranked Kimmich's Heady Topper IPA the number-one beer in the world. RateBeer.com ranked Hill Farmstead the number-one brewery in the world. And both websites rated Lawson's Finest Liquids world-class. The trio's beverages, which are symphonic in flavor, rarely travel outside of northern Vermont.

Kimmich, who moved from his native Pittsburgh to the Green Mountain State in 1994 to learn the brewing trade from Greg Noonan, began to make his reputation back in 2003. That's when he and his wife, Jen, opened the Alchemist Pub & Brewery in downtown Waterbury, a few miles from the ski resort town of Stowe. You didn't just happen upon the Alchemist; you made a pilgrimage to it. When Kimmich released Heady Topper, an 8-percent-alcohol double IPA with impossibly intricate layers of hop character, he figured he was going out on a limb. "I wasn't sure if

Shaun Hill of Hill Farmstead, courtesy of Bob M. Montgomery Images.

people would like the hoppy beers that I like." In fact, they went mad for it. For the brief duration that a keg of the stuff would last, some customers would order a glass and slyly empty the contents into a take-home container.

When John and Jen made plans to build a production brewery, they decided that Heady Topper would be their only product. The plan was to run both businesses simultaneously, until disaster struck the pub in the form of Tropical Storm Irene in August 2011. The basement brewery was flooded, and insurance would not cover the damage. The couple simultaneously cursed their bad luck and counted their blessings. At least they had the new Alchemist Brewery; they would pour their hearts into that. They made a bold statement by not only brewing just one beer, but by putting that beer in a silver tallboy emblazoned with a foamy-haired tippler who wouldn't look out of place on the cover of High Times. And get this: you are instructed right on the packaging to "Drink from the can!"

On a muddy day in March, a steady stream of customers lined up at the Alchemist to buy a maximum allotment of two cases of Heady Topper for seventy-two dollars each. Among them were two friends who had driven up from Pennsylvania. Kimmich is not sure what to make of the celebrity that has befallen him in tiny Waterbury. It's weird, he says, to go to brew fests and be swarmed by "guys who have beer crushes on you." In its first two years, the Alchemist expanded production 600 percent. It recently grew to a capacity of nine thousand barrels per year, and Kimmich says that's enough. His ambition does not include sending Heady Topper to every beer bar from Boston to D.C. Unlike his predecessors in the 1990s, he doesn't have to.

That is also pretty much Shaun Hill's take on things. He cut his brewing teeth at The Shed brewpub in Stowe after homebrewing his way through Haverford College, where he studied philosophy. He moved on to a stint at the Trout River Brewing Company in Lyndonville and then took off to Denmark in 2008 to be a guest brewer at Nørrebro Bryghus —one of a new wave of craft breweries in Europe. There, he introduced a barrel-aging program and brewed three beers—an imperial stout, a barleywine, and a sour ale—that won two gold medals and a silver medal at the 2010 World Beer Cup. The awards were auspiciously announced just as Hill returned to his family's one-hundred-acre homestead in Greensboro Bend, forty miles from the Canadian border, to build his own brewery.

Hill Farmstead brews received almost instant praise from connoisseurs, who broadcast their excitement over the Web and social media. The way Hill names and packages his beer is part of its allure. Brews in the permanent lineup are named for family members who for eight generations have inhabited the land on which Hill Farmstead sits. Edward, the top seller, is an American pale ale named for Hill's grandfather. Specialty brews are named for philosophical works. Michel Foucault's *Madness and Civilization* inspired a series of blends of dark, strong beers that have been aging in wine or bourbon barrels. Hill says that his goblet-in-an-hourglass insignia comes from an old sign for the tavern that his great-great grandfather Aaron Hill once ran. It looks similar to the way Hill's beers taste: rooted in tradition but distinctly modern.

Like Kimmich, Hill appreciates the glowing recognition his talent has received but is puzzled by its magnitude. His long, dirt driveway is often clogged with the cars of beer pilgrims who patiently wait in line to fill a growler or buy bottles of beer. Sometimes people wander into his house next door looking for a bathroom. Hill has plans to expand—to a maximum production of 3,500 barrels annually. "I don't want to be a larger brewer. I just sort of want to build a playground," he said in an interview for *Vanity Fair*.

Sean Lawson's output is even smaller than that of Kimmich or Hill. He's what the industry calls a nanobrewer. After homebrewing for eighteen years for friends and family who urged him to go pro, he finally built a little barn-like brewery next to his house in Warren (near Waterbury) modeled after a maple sugarhouse. He doesn't offer tours

Shoveling grain and adding hops, courtesy of Notch Brewing.

or retail sales. It's all he can do to supply cult favorites like Double Sunshine IPA—laced with so much herbal hop character you could practically smoke it—and Maple Tripple—a strong ale brewed each spring from maple sap and aged for one year—to the Warren Store and a handful of bars when he's not peddling his own wares at the Montpelier Farmer's Market.

In a world where thousands of breweries are competing for shelf space, brewers must make good beer and stand out in some way. As the success of Lawson, Hill, and Kimmich demonstrates, it helps to push the envelope—in strength, hoppiness, or style. It also helps to be limited. No beer is more desirable than the one you can't get.

———◇———

Chris Lohring didn't so much want to stand out in a crowded marketplace as brew beers he liked. Facing boozy IPAs wherever he went, he longed for a low-alcohol brew made with as much care as the extreme beers that dominated BeerAdvocate's Top 250 list. Where were the Czech-style pilsners, the mild, black lagers, or even the IPAs that had loads of hop character but under 5 percent alcohol? When Lohring goes out, he says, "I want to have three beers—but not three beers at 7 percent.

"The session beer space was being ignored. It got to the point where I started homebrewing. I loathe homebrewing." Lohring would rather make beer in a professional facility, as he did between 1994 and 2001 as co-owner of the Tremont Brewery in Charlestown, Massachusetts. He and partner Alex Reveliotty produced a crisp, dry English pale ale that made a lot of Boston-area beer drinkers happy. When it came time for them to expand, they couldn't find the financing and became yet another victim of the great shakeout at the turn of the new millennium. Tremont contract-brewed at Shipyard until 2005, when the bigger brewery finally acquired it.

For the next five years, Lohring turned his back on the brewing scene. Having studied engineering at the Worcester Polytechnic Institute and business at Northeastern University, he worked for a product-design incubator and traveled the world, viewing new technologies three or four years before the consumer did. But, he says, "I missed brewing terribly."

When he launched Notch Brewing in 2010, he relived the experience of being ahead of consumers. His flagship, Notch Pils, a crisp and hoppy Czech-style lager with 4 percent alcohol—about the same as in a less flavorful lite beer—was slow to catch on.

"It took a little longer for people to come around to session beer," Lohring says. "Consumers didn't understand. Those in their twenties have been raised on high-alcohol beer. My demographic is more mature—they have life responsibilities. When I understood that, that's when Notch started to have a little more success." Lohring is a tenant brewer, producing over 5,000 barrels of beer a year at Ipswich Ale Brewery and the Two Roads Brewing Company, with plans to build his own brewery, beer garden, and tap room in Salem, Massachusetts.

Brewing low-alcohol beers takes skill. They are subtle and balanced; there are no big flavors for flaws to hide behind. Lohring has made a beer as low as 2.8 percent—Notch Tafelbier, a Belgian table beer traditionally enjoyed by the whole family at mealtime. His Left of the Dial IPA (4.3 percent), named for where alternative radio resides on the frequency spectrum, debunks the notion that an IPA must be strong. Lohring wrote in a blog post that it tastes "like an IPA, but without any cloying sweetness and booze that fatigues and gets in the way of multiple pints and extended good times."

Demand for session beer is growing nationwide. Beer and spirits writer Lew Bryson of Philadelphia both encourages and chronicles the trend on his Session Beer Project blog. He notes that low-alcohol beers have emerged recently from bigger craft breweries, such as Boulevard of Missouri, Odell of Colorado, Deschutes of Oregon, Founders of Michigan, and Stone of San Diego. As far as Bryson knows, however, Notch is the only American brewery to dedicate itself entirely to session beers.

———◆———

It's heartening to see some of the seasoned brewers of the 1990s reviving their careers and making the New England scene richer in return. In the most recent of these comebacks, Tod Mott has found a new home for his many recipes: a new brewery that he is launching in Kittery, Maine, called Tributary. These brewers savor their success with one eye fixed on the rear-view mirror, because they remember what a bubble looks like. When the subject comes up, many brewers utter some variation of, "There are too many beers out there"—even while they busily add new beers to their portfolios. That's the challenge of the current climate: your beer has to be high-quality, and you must constantly offer something new (the Alchemist being the rare exception to the latter rule).

Craft brewers seem both invigorated and intimidated by this reality. Some are exasperated by it. David Geary, whose flagship pale ale remains as balanced as when it debuted almost thirty years ago, grouchily refers to the multitudes of extreme beers as "'Oh, look at me' beers." And yet he's responsible for one of the first extreme beers: Hampshire Special Ale (7 percent alcohol), which was considered boozy when it came out in 1988 and was sought after by aficionados. But there were fewer aficionados back then, and they weren't broadcasting their appreciation on Facebook and Twitter and driving up from Pennsylvania because this big, malty beer from Maine made the BeerAdvocate Top 250 list. Hampshire Special Ale is still special, but it has a lot more company than it used to.

You might think there are too many beers on package-store shelves. Or you might think that the craft segment still has plenty of room to expand—even after years of double-digit growth, it still only accounts for 18 percent of malt beverage sales. Regardless, you understand that the world of beer in New England is a lot different now than when the first bottles of Geary's rolled off the line in 1986. The region's brewers are proliferating, offering beer drinkers more and better products than ever before. There are more venues for craft beer and more ways to promote it. There is also a lot more noise over which brewers must make themselves heard. To succeed, they have to be just as crafty as

Courtesy of Notch Brewing.

the Puritans who substituted corn and molasses for scarce malt, the Industrial Era moguls who bobbed and weaved around temperance reform, and the early microbrewers who scavenged equipment and faced indifference from the average Bud drinker.

Up until Prohibition, almost all beer was local. The mass-produced, national (and now global) brands we all grew up with are still new in the context of beer's seven-thousand-year history—and they will likely, given economies of scale and the wonders of the modern supply chain, remain the norm for the forseeable future. But, in a throwback to the days of Hanley's, Haffenreffer, and Hull, New Englanders' consumption of local beer continues to grow. The likes of Pretty Things Beer and Ale Project and Hill Farmstead have proved that there is a voracious demand in the region for good beer brewed close by. Small breweries are opening in towns that never had them before. More Yankee ales and lagers are flowing through beer-bar taps once dominated by products from Colorado and California. If Samuel Adams were alive today, he'd be delighted. Remember when he begged his fellow colonists to brew their own beer so that they didn't have to "be beholden to Foreigners for a Credible Liquor?" Almost two hundred and fifty years later, New England's brewers are fulfilling that wish once more.

ACKNOWLEDGEMENTS

This book would not exist without the support of my family and Eric Martinson, for whom I am deeply grateful.

I naturally owe thanks to Nicole Vecchiotti of Union Park Press, who was convinced I would make a good author. She and her team, Deepa Chungi, Shelby Larsson, and Caitlin Cullerot, helped my words sound and look nice, and, crucially, wind up in the hands of readers.

Before any words went down on the page, Lew Bryson, Gregg Glaser, and Stephanie Schorow gave me crucial encouragement and advice.

For inspiration, I imagined David Wondrich, Wayne Curtis, Michael Jackson (the late British beer writer), and Sarah Vowell looking over my shoulder.

Sue Blake provided a lovely space for me to write. Bob Sabbag, Jill McDonough, Josey Packard, and Kate Palmer talked me off the ledge when necessary.

Ron Pattinson and Michael Reiskind generously shared their knowledge of the history of beer styles and breweries. Ken Ostrow, Joe and Karen Carey, and Rus Hammer graciously invited me into their homes to look at vintage beer memorabilia.

The staff at the Boston Athenaeum and the Wellfleet Public Library were supportive during the hours I spent at those places writing and researching. At the University of Michigan Clements Library, Diana Mankowski tracked down rare documents for me.

During my travels around New England, I enjoyed the hospitality of Lucky and Toby Hollander, Gretchen and Alex McDonald, and Chris Sheridan.

Many other friends and colleagues cheered me on. You know who you are, and I hope to enjoy a pint with you all. Let's raise our glasses to the brewers of New England, whose soul-fortifying liquids inspire our conversations as well as the words on these pages.

SOURCES

CHAPTER 1: WATER

Bradford, William, *Of Plimouth Plantation*

John Winthrop's letters

Wood, William, *New England's Prospect*

Markham, Gervayse, *The English Housewife*

Baron, Stanley, *Brewed in America: A History of Beer and Ale In the United States,* Little Brown, 1962

Smith, Gregg, *Beer in America: The Early Years—1587-1840*, Brewers Publications, 1998

Bennett, Judith M., *Ale, Beer and Brewsters in England*, Oxford University Press, 1996

Thomann, Gallus, *American Beer: Glimpses of Its History and Description of Its Manufacture*, United States Brewers Association, 1909

Carmichael, Zachary A., *Fit Men: New England Tavern Keepers*, Miami University, 2009

Earle, Alice Morse, *Margaret Winthrop*, C. Scribner's Sons, 1985

Vowell, Sarah, *The Wordy Shipmates*, Riverhead Hardcover, 2008

An Historic Guide to Cambridge, Daughters of the American Revolution, 1907

Battista, Carolyn, "New Haven, a City of Beer Making (Until Prohibition)," *New York Times*, Dec 13, 1998

Records Relating to the Early History of Boston, Volume 2, Municipal Printing Office, 1900

Adams, Nathaniel, *Annals of Portsmouth*, C. Norris, 1825

"Puritanism," *History.com*

"Roger Williams," *History.com*

Anderson, Robert Charles, "Our Family Genealogy Pages," Upshall

"Nicholas Upsal," *Family Record.net*

"Upsall, Nicholas," Dorchester Athenaeum

Conroy, David W., *In Public Houses*, University of North Carolina Press, 1995

CHAPTER 2: MALT AND HOPS

Russell Howard S., *A Long, Deep Furrow*, University Press of New England, 1976

Weaver, John, "Barley in the United States: A Historical Sketch," *Geographical Review*, January 1943, Vol. 33 No. 1

Walcott, Robert R., "Husbandry in Colonial New England," *The New England Quarterly* Vol. 9, No. 2 (June 1936)

Baron, *Brewed in America*

Smith, *Beer in America*

Bishop, John Leander; Troxell Freedley, Edwin; Young, Edward, *A History of American Manufactures from 1608 to 1860*, E. Young & Company, 1864

Lord Gordon, Adam, "Journal of an Officer Who Traveled in America and the West Indies in 1764 and 1765," Newton D. Mereness (editor) *Travels in the American Colonies*, The MacMillan Company, 1916

Deane, Samuel, *The New England Farmer, Or Georgical Dictionary*, Wells and Lilly, 1822

"Diary of Samuel Sewall: 1674-1729," Collections of the Massachusetts Historical Society, 1878-1882

Sewall, Samual, *The History of Woburn, Middlesex County, Mass.*, Wiggin and Lunt Publishers, 1868

Tomlan, Michael A., *Tinged with Gold: Hop Culture in the United States*, University of Georgia Press, 1992

Curtis, Wayne, *And a Bottle of Rum: A History of the New World in Ten Cocktails*, Broadway Books, 2007

Flint, Daniel, "The Hop Industry in California," *Transactions of the California State Agricultural Society During the Year 1891*, A.J. Johnston, 1892

Gregory, Tom, *History of Yolo County, California*, Historic Record Company, 1913

Interview with Andrea Stanley, March 2013

Interview with Will Meyers, March 2013

Interview with Bill Goldfarb, March 2013

Interview with Alex McDonald and Butch Heilshorn, March 2013

Krakowski, Adam, *A Bitter Past: Hop Farming in Nineteenth Century Vermont*, 2010

Fimrite, Peter, "Joseph Owades -- brewmaster, created light beer," *San Francisco Chronicle*, December 20, 2005

Roach, John, "Eight Ancient Drinks Uncorked By Science," *NBCNews.com*, December 17, 2009

CHAPTER 3: BARRELS

Baron, *Brewed in America*

Smith, *Beer in America*

The Mariners' Museum Website

Taylor, Alan, *American Colonies: The Settling of North America,* Penguin Books, 2002

Keir, Malcolm, "Some Influences of the Sea Upon the Industries of New England," *The Geographical Review of the American Geographical Society,* 1918

Speech of the Hon. Daniel Webster, on the Subject of Slavery: Delivered in the United States Senate, on Thursday, March 7, 1850

Conover, George, S., *History of Bedford, NH,* J. W. Lewis, 1885

Delo, David M., *Peddlers and Post Traders: The Army Settler on the Frontier,* University of Utah Press, 1992

Stevens, Benjamin F., "Some of the Old Inns and Taverns of Boston," *The Bostonian,* Vol. II, April-September 1895

Goold, Nathan, "Falmouth Neck in the Revolution," *Collections of the Maine Historical Society,* 1896

Bennington Museum, Bennington, VT

The Encyclopedia Britannica, "Green Mountain Boys," 2014.

Smallwood, Frank, *Thomas Chittenden: Vermont's First Statesman,* New England Pr Inc, 1997

Website for Town of Brooklyn, CT

Livingston, William Farrand, *Israel Putnam: Pioneer, Ranger and Major-general, 1718-1790,* The Knickerbocker Press, 1901

Larned, Ellen Douglas, *History of Windham County, Connecticut: 1760-1880,* Charles Hamilton (printers),1880

Adams, Charles Francis, *Three Episodes of Massachusetts History, Vol. II,* 1892

Belknap, Jeremy, *The History of New Hampshire, Vol. III,* J. Mann and J. K. Remick, 1812

Russell, *A Long, Deep Furrow*

Garvin, Donna-Belle; Garvin, James L., *On the Road North of Boston: New Hampshire Taverns and Turnpikes, 1700-1900,* New Hampshire Historical Society, 1988

Mereness, Newton Dennison (editor), "Journal of Lord Adam Gordon" in *Travels in the American Colonies,* The Macmillan Co. of Canada LTD, 1916

Interview with Steve Wood, March 2013

Watson, Ben, *Cider, Hard and Sweet: History, Traditions and Making Your Own,* Countryman Press, 1999

Collins, Jim, "History: Hard Cider in New England," *Yankee Magazine,* September 2010

Browning, Frank, "Adventures of Cider Man," *Food & Wine,* November 2001

Hughes, Christopher, "Three New England Ciders to Watch (and Drink)," *Boston Magazine,* November 12, 2012.

Stowe, John M.; Bennett, William, *History of the Town of Hubbardston, Worcester County, Mass,* 1881

Field, Edward, *The Colonial Tavern: A Glimpse of New England Town Life in the Seventeenth and Eighteenth Centuries,* Preston and Rounds,1897

Estes, David Foster, *The History of Holden, Massachusetts. 1684-1894,* C. F. Lawernce & Co, 1894

Damon, Samuel Chenery, *History of the Military Company of the Massachusetts Vol. III,* Oliver Ayer Roberts, 1898

Wriston, John C. Jr., *Vermont Inns and Taverns: Pre-Revolution to 1925,* Academy Books, 1991

Conroy, *In Public Houses*

CHAPTER 4: ICE AND STEAM

Baron, Stanley, "One Hundred Years of Brewing," a supplement to *The Western Brewer,* 1903

Stanley Baron, *Brewed in America,* 1962

Schorow, Stephanie, *Drinking Boston,* Union Park Press, 2012

Brown, Richard D.; Tager, Jack, *Massachusetts: A Concise History,* University of Massachusetts Press, 2000

Ward, Andrew Henshaw, *A Genealogical History of the Rice Family: Descendants of Deacon Edmund Rice,* C. Benjamin Richardson, 1858.

Henry Martyn Wheeler, *Geneology of Some of the Descendants of Obadiah Wheeler of Concord,* F. P. Rice, 1898

"Benjamin Thaxter Obituary," *Boston Evening Transcript,* September 6, 1886

Bowditch, Nathanial, I., *A History of the Massachusetts General Hospital,* 1851

Johnson, Rossiter; Brown, John Howard, *The Twentieth Century Biographical Dictionary of Notable Americans,* Biographical Society, 1904

Edwards, R. A. R., *Words Made Flesh: Nineteenth-Century Deaf Education and the Growth of Deaf Culture,* NYU Press, 2012

Boston Beer Company Collection, 1828-1836, William L. Clements Library, University of Michigan

Letter Dec 4, 1885 to Caleb W. Loring, trustee of Boston Beer Co. from D.H. Tully, Jr. (Boston Athenaeum collection)

Stevens, Peter F., *Hidden History of the Boston Irish,* The History Press, 2008

"Commercial and Financial New England Illustrated," *The Boston Herald,* 1906

Sawyer, Timothy Thompson, *Old Charlestown: Historical, Biographical, Reminiscent,* James H. West Company, 1902

Eliot, Samuel Atkins, *Biographical History of Massachusetts,* Massachusetts Biographical Society, 1911

Toomey, Daniel P.; Quinn, Thomas Charles, *Massachusetts of Today: A Memorial of the State, Historical and Biographical*, Columbia Publishing Company, 1892

"Boston Beer Company," Historic American Engineering Record No. MA-138

Gray, George Arthur, *The Descendants of George Holmes of Roxbury: 1594-1908*, David Clapp & Son, 1908

Theberge, Greg, "The History of the Brewing Industry in Rhode Island," (slide presentation) 2012

Winslow, Richard Elliott, *Frank Jones of New Hampshire: A Capitalist and a Politician During the Gilded Age*, University of New Hampshire, 1965

Brighton, Ray, *Frank Jones: King of the Alemakers*, Peter E. Randall Publishers, 1976

"Back to the Future," *The Portsmouth Herald*, April 5, 1992

Cornell, Martyn, "The Forgotten Story of London Porters," *The Zythophile : Beer Then and Now*, November 2, 2007

Wondrich, David, "The Darkest Beer," *Esquire,* March 23, 2012

Stack, Martin H., "A Concise History of America's Brewing Industry," EH.net, July 4, 2013

"New Haven, A City of Beermaking (Until Prohibition)," *New York Times*, December 13, 1998

"New Haven Brews Up History," *Hartford Courant*, May 14, 1998

"Wealthy Philip Fresenius Cuts Relatives Off in Will and Leaves Estate to Widow," *Bridgeport Herald*, February 27, 1910

Anderson, Will, *Beer New England*, 1988

Cushman; Hammer; Lang; McMurtery; McMurtery; Ostrow; Purvis; Theberge; Theberge; *New England Breweriana*, 2000

"Beer Here—Well It Was Here, But Only for a Few Decades," *Hartford Courant*, September 26, 2007

"Springfield Armory," *Encyclopedia Britannica*

"Administration Watch-Dogs Keep Use of Harvard Name Under Control," *Harvard Crimson*, April 8, 1999

Anderson, Will, *The Great State of Maine Beer Book*, 1996

Richardson, Whit, "The Great Rum Riot," *DownEast*, 2010

CHAPTER 5: ALCOHOL

Barr, Andrew, *Drink: A Social History of America*, Carroll and Graf Publishers, 1999

Baron, *Brewed in America*

Thomann, *American Beer*

Duis, Perry, *The Saloon: Public Drinking in Chicago and Boston, 1880-1920*, University of Illinois Press, 1998

Baron, *"One Hundred Years of Brewing,"* a supplement to *The Western Brewer,* 1903

Okrent, Daniel, *Last Call: The Rise and Fall of Prohibition*, Scribner, 2010

Johnson, Allen (editor), *Dictionary of American Biography*, Vol. V., Charles Scribners' Sons, 1929

Dow, Neal, *The Reminiscences of Neal Dow*, The Evening Express Publishing Company, 1898

Ostrander, Gilman, *The Prohibition Movement in California: 1848-1933*, University of California Press, 1957

Richardson, Whit, "The Great Rum Riot," *Down East*, 2010

Daniels, William Haven, *The Temperance Reform and Its Great Reformers*, Nelson and Phillips, 1878

Vermont State Archives, "Statewide Referendum 1903: Regulating the Traffic in Intoxicating Liquor"

"The Vienna Brewery," Boston Landmarks Commission, 1998

"Report of Chief of Police," Documents of the City of Boston for the Year 1873, Vol. 1

Mukerji, Chandra; Schudson, Michael (editors), *Rethinking Popular Culture: Contemporary Perspectives in Cultural Studies*, University of California Press, 1991

Thomann, Gallus, *Documentary History of the United States Brewers' Association*, United States Brewers' Association, 1896

"Non-partisanship: Or, Do Not Take Temperance Into Politics," By A Friend of Temperance, 1888

Geer's Harford City Directory, 1903

Bielawa, Michael J., *Wicked Bridgeport*, History Press, 2012

CHAPTER 6: BOTTLES AND CANS

Baron, *Brewed in America*

Brewers Almanac 2013 (Beer Institute)

Acitelli, Tom, *The Audacity of Hops: The History of America's Craft Beer Revolution*, Chicago Review Press, 2013

Tremblay and Tremblay, *The U.S. Brewing Industry*, MIT Press, 2005

New England Breweriana, Schiffer Book for Collectors, 2001

Anderson, *Beer New England*, 1988

Discussion with Will Anderson, *BeerCanHistory.com*, 2009

Interview with Will Anderson, March 2013

Smith, Andrew F. (editor), *The Oxford Companion to American Food and Drink*, Oxford University Press, USA, 2009

Breuer, William B., *J. Edgar Hoover and His G-Men*, Praeger, 1995

Windham, Ryder, *You Know You're in Rhode Island When...*, Globe Pequot, 2006

"Our county and its people: A descriptive and biographical history of Bristol County, Massachusetts," *Fall River News and Taunton Gasette*, 1899

Turley, Hazel, *Narragansett Brewing Company*, Arcadia Publishing, 2007

Marquard, Bryan, "Theodore Haffenreffer, 91; ran brewery," *The Boston Globe*, January 15, 2009

"Rudolf F. Haffenreffer 3d, Industrialist, 88," *Associated Press*, May 1, 1991

"August Haffenreffer, 94; concocted potent 'Green Death' beer," *The Boston Globe*, August 30, 2010

Rhode Island Heritage Hall of Fame

Morton, John Fass, *Backstory in Blue: Ellington at Newport '56*, Rutgers University Press, 2008

Reiskind, Micael, "Boston's Lost Breweries," Jamaica Plain Historical Society, March 25, 2006

"Enterprise Brewery Co. Began Operations 1898," *Fall River Herald News*, September 19, 1953

Moniz, William, "Flood unearths bottle tied to city's brewing past," *Fall River Spirit*, July 29, 2010

Interview with Nick Shields, July 2013

Interview with Jeff Browning, March 2013

Interview with Bill Anderson, March 2013

Interview with Sean Larkin, March 2013

Interview with Jim Crooks, March 2013

Weisstuch, Liza, "A beloved beer bubbles back," *The Boston Globe*, June 4, 2010

narragansettbeer.com

Turley, *Narragansett Brewing Company*

Donnis, Ian, "The Beer Boom," *The Providence Phoenix*, Aug 25, 2005

falstaffbrewing.com

Olmstead, Larry, "Craft Beers Say Hello Cans, Goodbye Bottles: An Aluminum Revolution," *Forbes*, May, 1, 2013

Quinn-Szcesuil, Julia, "Embracing a can-do attitude," *The Boston Globe*, April 18, 2012

Interview with Rob Leonard and Matt Westfall, March 2013

CHAPTER 7: YEAST

Acitelli, *The Audacity of Hops*

Holl, John, *Massachusetts Breweries*, Stackpole Books, 2012

American Homebrewers Association

Interview with Pat Baker, July 2013

Interview with Mark Larrow, July 2013

Interview with Steve Stroud, March 2013

Interview with Nancy Crosby, July 2013

Bjcp.org

Garrett, Oliver; Colicchio, Thomas, *The Oxford Companion to Beer,* Oxford University Press, USA, 2011

Reid, Peter V. K., "A Brief History of Imported Beer," *Brewing History Research Program*, March 31, 2004

David Geary interview in The Commons, 2012

Anderson, Will, *The Great State of Maine Beer Book*

Johnson, Steve, *On Tap New England*, Tap Publications, 1994

Interview with Phil Leinhart, July 2013

Interview with Phil Markowski, March 2013

Interview with Jim Lee, July 2013

Interview with Jim Koch, April 2013

Interview with David Geary, March 2013

Interview with Alan Pugsley, March 2013

Interview with Dan Kramer, March 2013

Bryson, Lew, "Ringwood: Like It or Leave It," *Massachusetts Beverage Business Journal*, June 2001

Eng, Dinah, "Jim Koch: Samuel Adams's Beer Revolutionary," *CNN Money*, March 21, 2013.

CHAPTER 8: FERMENTATION

Dzen, Gary, "Harpoon Renovation Warms Welcome for Visitors," *The Boston Globe*, January, 15 2013

Acitelli, *The Audacity of Hops*

Kamp, David, *The United States of Arugula: How We Became a Gourmet Nation*, Clarskon Potter, 2006

Brewers Association

BeerAdvocate.com

Fleischer, Chris, "On Tap: Larger Brewers Think Small to Keep Innovation Flowing," *Valley News*, April, 24 2013

Brewers Association List of Domestic Non-Craft Brewers

Nolte, Jason, "10 Craft Beers That Aren't," *The Street*, January 1, 2013

HarpoonBrewery.com

Gorski, Eric, "Magic Hat Brewing Company Beer Arrives in Colorado," *Denver Post*, January 23, 2013

Bromage, Andy, "Magic Touch," *Seven Days: Vermont's Independent Voice*, November 2, 2011

"Through SHARP, Long Trail Brewing Company sets craft-brewing industry's workplace safety benchmark," United States Department of Labor

"Berkshire Brewing Company releases signature Pale Ale in cans," *WWLP Western Massachusetts*, August 2013

BerkshireBrewingCompany.com

"New NH Brewery to Open by End of Year," *Associated Press*, June, 23 2013

Ward, Jackie, "Allagash Continues Brewing Up Success," *WCSH Portland*, February, 4 2013,

"Behind the Brew: Ray McNeill, McNeill's Brewing," *BrewByBike.com*, June 16, 2013

Bryson, Lew, "Long Trail's Pherson," *Massachusetts Beverage Business Journal*, October 2004

Machalaba, Daniel, "The Golden Years, Literally," *The Wall Street Journal*, May 30, 2012

Latif, Ray, "Long Trail President Steps Down as Brewery Continues to Expand Operations, Footprint," *Brewbound.com*, January 8, 2013

Donelly, John, "Vermont Brewery Sings the Blues; It Can't Get Started," *Plattsburgh Press-Republican*, January 5, 1987

Rosenwein, Rifka, "Obituary: Despite Ale's Success, Brewery Loses Out," *Inc.*, October 1, 2001

Calta, Marialisa, "Soon, Catamount Amber, a 'British' Pale Ale from Vermont," *The New York Times*, December 3, 1986

"Great American Salvage," *ReclaimedHome.com*, November 8, 2011

Curtain, Jack, "Black and Bitter: True Origins of Black IPA," *Ale Street News*, August 5, 2010

Interview with Phil Bannatyne, March 2013

Interview with Nancy Noonan, July 2013

Interview with Jerome Noonan, June 2013

Interview with Peter Egelston, March 2013

Interview with Janet Egelston, March 2013

Interview with Alan Pugsley, March 2013

Interview with Tod Mott, March 2013

Interview with David Geary, March 2013

Interview with Tony Lubold, August 2013

Interview with Paul Sayler, March 2013

Interview with Steve Israel, September 2013

Interview with Ed Stebbins and Richard Pfeffer, March 2013

Boston Beer Company Limited Partnership, v. Slesar Bros. Brewing Company, Inc., Boston Beer Works, United States Court of Appeals, First Circuit, 9 F.3d 175, Heard Oct. 5, 1993 Decided Nov. 16, 1993

CHAPTER 9: REFERMENTATION

BeerInstitute.org

BrewersAssociation.org

BeerMe.com

BeerAdvocate.com

RealBeer.com

Hamburg, Steve, "Cask Ale: Keeping it Real," *All About Beer*, May 1, 2010

Gee, Brandon, "N.H. Law Gives Nanobreweries a Larger Standing," *The Boston Globe*, February 25, 2013

Shikes, Jonathan, "Todd Alström talks about Beer Advocate's influence and his move to Denver," *Denver Westword*, August 6, 2013

Carter, Spike, "An Interview with Shaun Hill, Brewmaster at Hill Farmstead, the 'Best Brewery in the World,'" *Vanity Fair*, April 25, 2013

Dunbar, Bathany M., "In Greensboro: Hill Farmstead Brewery expansion wins approval," *The Chronicle Online*, January 23, 2013

Goff, Rachel, "Lawson's Finest Liquids celebrates five years," *The Valley Reporter*, March 21, 2013

Interview with Rob Tod, March 2013

Interview with Daniel Kleban, March 2013

Interview with Chris Lohring, October 2013

Interview with Martha Holley-Simpson, March 2013

Interview with Dann Paquette, September 2013

Interview with John Kimmich, March 2013

Interview with Shaun Hill, March 2013

Interview with Tod Mott, March 2013

Interview with David Geary, March 2013

INDEX